The Moody Guide to BIBLE LANDS

by Tim Dowley
Illustrations and maps by Richard Scott

Moody Press
Chicago

Contents

If we read the Bible from beginning to end – from the book of Genesis to the book of Revelation – we take a long journey through space and time. We start in Mesopotamia and pass through Palestine into Egypt. We leave Egypt for the Wilderness and finally enter the Promised Land. We travel from Jerusalem to Babylon, to Antioch, Corinth, Athens, and Rome – and finally to the New Jerusalem.

The story of the Bible takes place in real places and among historical people. The lands of the Bible are very varied: there are hot, dry deserts, bare mountains, and fertile river valleys.

This book is designed to help you understand the background against which the story of the Bible unfolds. The maps and illustrations follow the Old and New Testament accounts in roughly the order they come in the Bible.

The World of the Bible

Although the events of the Bible have world-wide importance, they took place in only a small area of the globe. Bible lands extend from Mesopotamia – 'the land between the rivers' – in the east to Italy and Spain in the west. But the story focuses particularly on the little land of Palestine at the eastern end of the Mediterranean Sea.

Palestine became important because it lay in the middle of the 'Fertile Crescent' – a great moon-shaped stretch of fertile land. Fringing the Arabian desert from Egypt up through Palestine and Syria, it then swings eastward down the valleys of the rivers Euphrates and Tigris to the Persian Gulf.

The Fertile Crescent

Only a small part of the world of the Bible could be cultivated. For instance, Egypt was a narrow land stretching along the banks of the river Nile; Mesopotamia a fertile land bounded by mountains. It was in these green strips that civilization began. Around 4500 BC people living there began to build irrigation ditches to water the land. People could settle and grow crops instead of wandering in search of food.

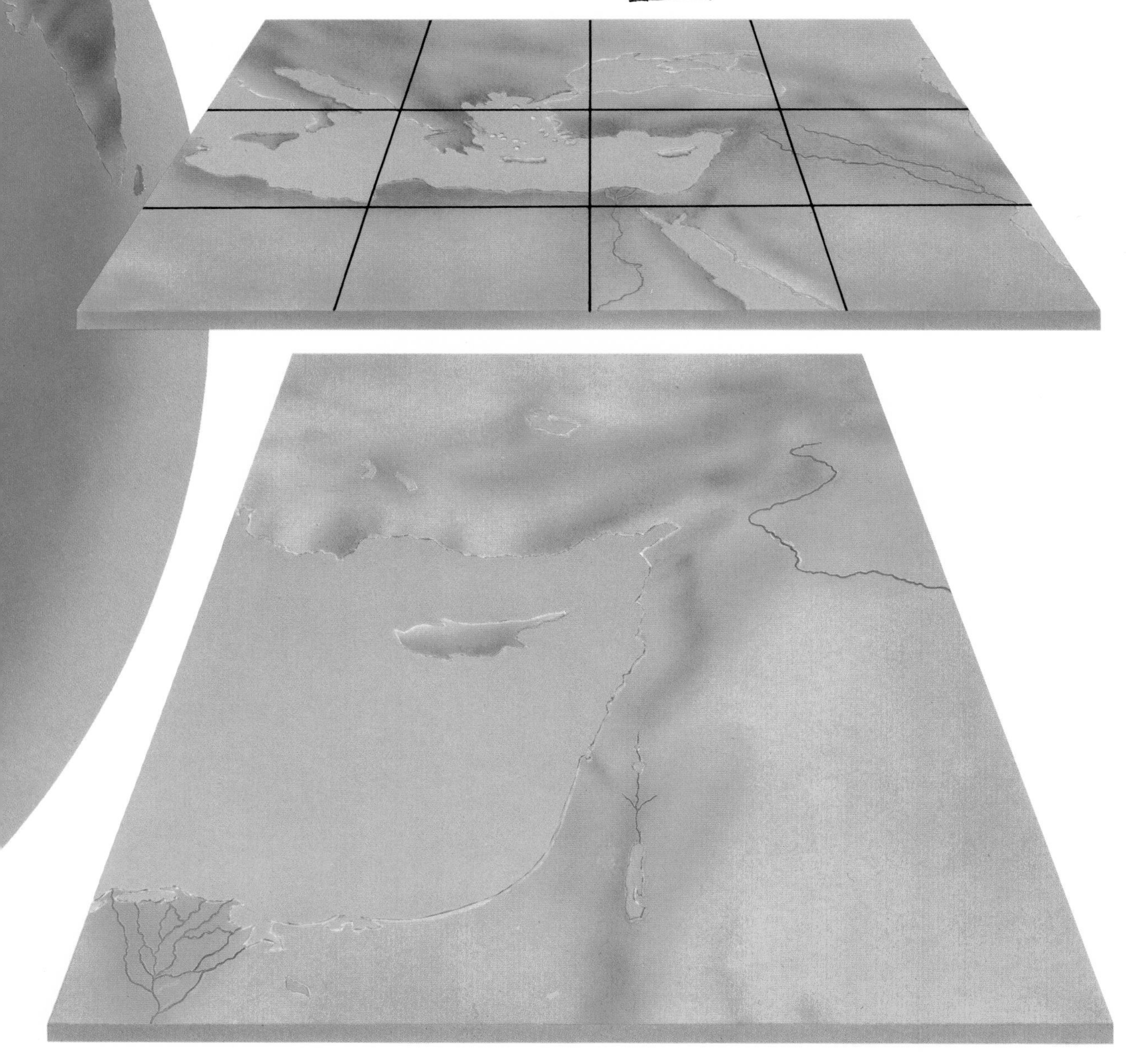

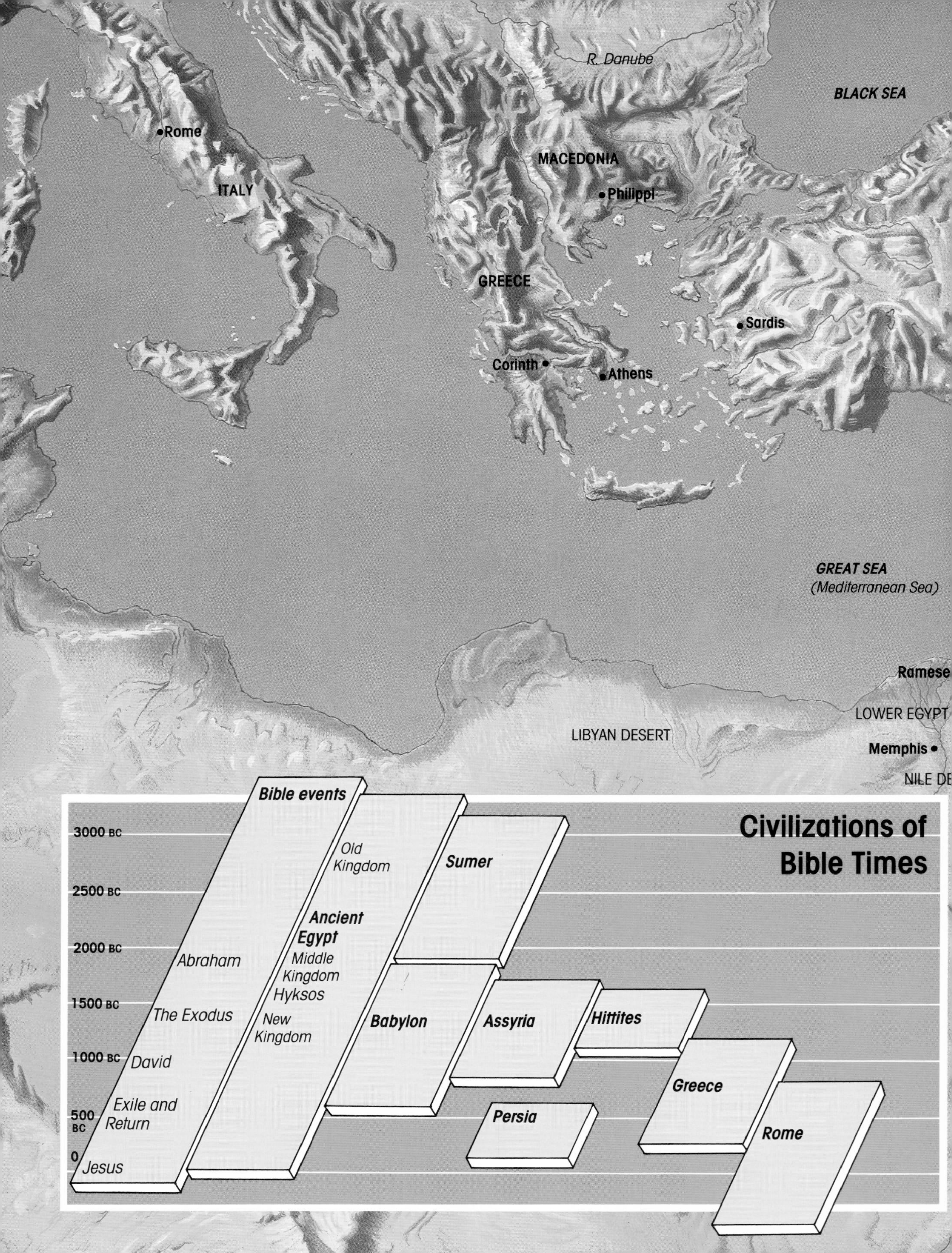

R. Danube
BLACK SEA
Rome
ITALY
MACEDONIA
Philippi
GREECE
Sardis
Corinth
Athens
GREAT SEA
(Mediterranean Sea)
Ramese
LOWER EGYPT
LIBYAN DESERT
Memphis
NILE DE
Civilizations of Bible Times
3000 BC
2500 BC
2000 BC
1500 BC
1000 BC
500 BC
0
Bible events
Abraham
The Exodus
David
Exile and Return
Jesus
Old Kingdom
Ancient Egypt
Middle Kingdom
Hyksos
New Kingdom
Sumer
Babylon
Assyria
Hittites
Greece
Persia
Rome

The Old Testament World

The peoples of the great river valleys of the Fertile Crescent became wealthy as a result of their irrigation schemes. But they were frequently attacked and defeated by the poor wandering people living in the deserts around them. Gradually the rulers of Egypt and Mesopotamia grew stronger. They began to reach out toward each other; but travellers and armies could not cross the dry Arabian desert. They had to travel through the green valleys of Syria and along the fertile coastal plains of Palestine. In this way Palestine, at the eastern end of the Mediterranean, became a vital land bridge between the lands of Egypt and Mesopotamia, and a crossroads of the ancient world.

Because people from Egypt and Mesopotamia travelled constantly across their lands, the peoples of Palestine and Syria were influenced by many of their customs and ideas.

Israel and the nations

Many great nations and empires rose and fell during the years covered in the Old Testament. As we have seen the ancient civilizations of Egypt and Mesopotamia were founded; later came the Assyrian, Babylonian, Persian, Greek and Roman empires.

Founding Fathers

Abraham's journeyings

Abraham, Isaac, Jacob, and Joseph were the great founding fathers of the Hebrew nation. God promised Abraham that he would have so many descendants that no-one would be able to count them.

Abraham's journeyings started in about 2100 BC when his father, Terah, left his home in the ancient city of Ur of the Chaldeans in the plain of Mesopotamia to travel north to the city of Haran.

After Terah died, God called Abraham to leave Haran to go to the land of Canaan. Although both Abraham and his wife, Sarah, were old and childless, God promised: 'I will make you into a great nation and I will bless you; I will make your name great, and you will be a blessing' (Genesis 12:2).

Abraham now became a nomad, travelling through barren desert country from one watering place to the next with his family, his flocks, and his herds. Finally they reached the land of Canaan, stretching about 150 miles from Mount Hermon in the north to the Negev desert in the south, and about fifty miles from the Mediterranean Sea in the west to the river Jordan in the east (Genesis 11–13).

Canaan

When he arrived in Canaan, Abraham built altars to God – at Shechem, near Bethel, and at Mamre. When famine came to Canaan, Abraham made a hasty trip to Egypt to buy food. Apart from this journey, he moved between Shechem, Mamre, and Bethel, leaving when his animals had exhausted the grazing at each place.

It was while Abraham was at Mamre that God fulfilled his promise that Sarah would bear a son. Isaac, their child, was to carry on Abraham's family line.

Abraham and Lot

Abraham did not travel alone from Haran; he was accompanied by his nephew Lot. As time passed, their flocks increased until it was no longer possible for them both to graze their animals in the same area.

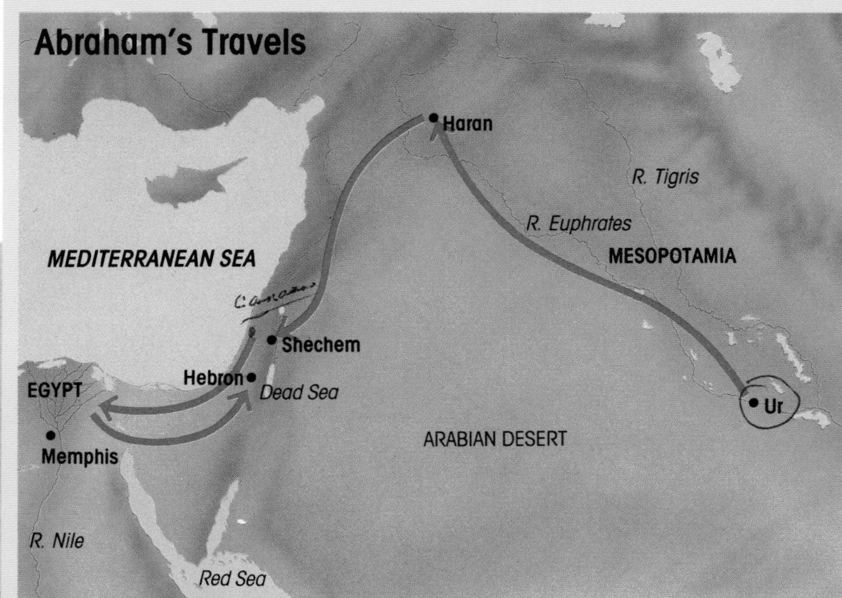

Hebron
Jacob buried here
Beer-sheba
EDOM

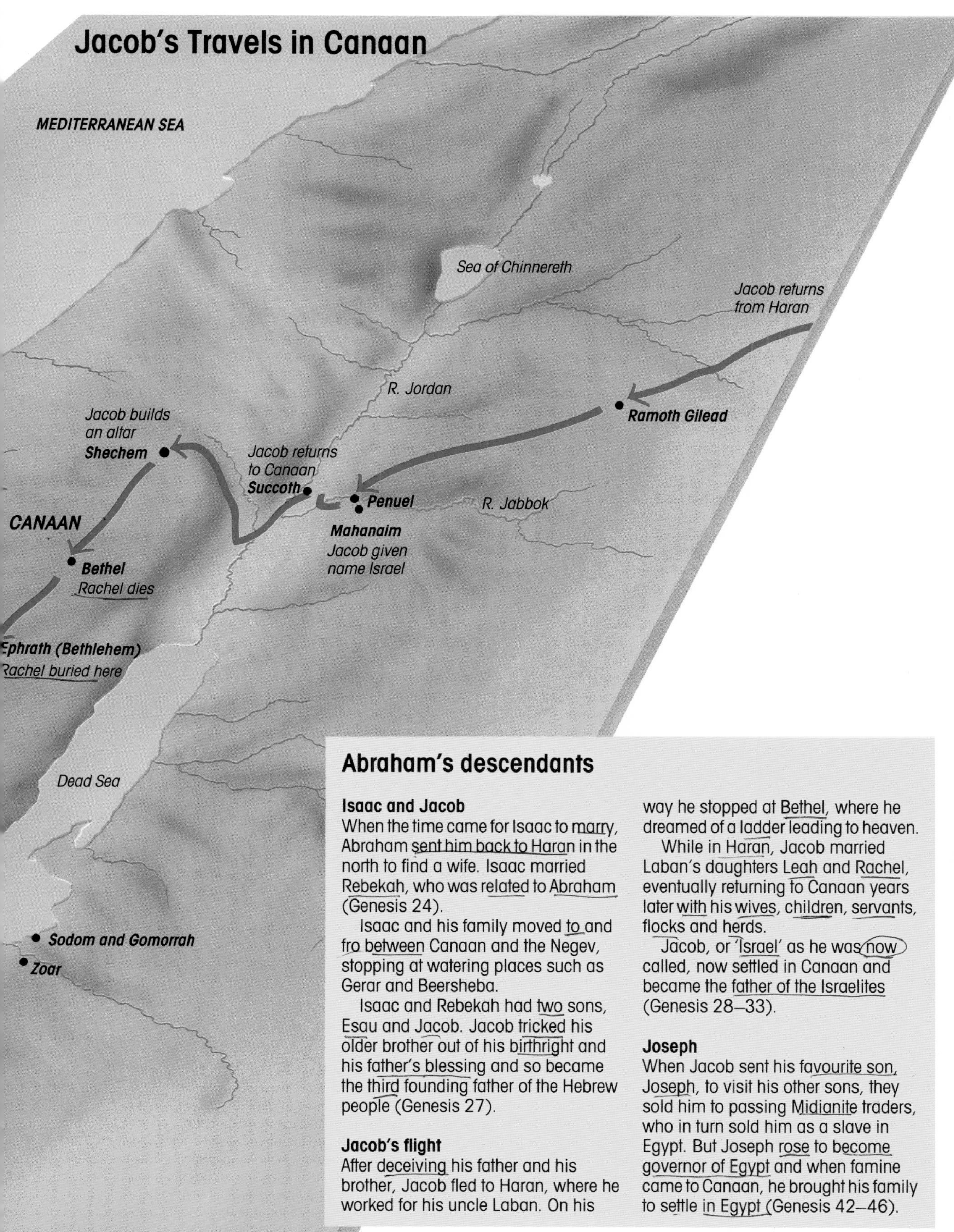

Abraham's descendants

Isaac and Jacob

When the time came for Isaac to marry, Abraham sent him back to Haran in the north to find a wife. Isaac married Rebekah, who was related to Abraham (Genesis 24).

Isaac and his family moved to and fro between Canaan and the Negev, stopping at watering places such as Gerar and Beersheba.

Isaac and Rebekah had two sons, Esau and Jacob. Jacob tricked his older brother out of his birthright and his father's blessing and so became the third founding father of the Hebrew people (Genesis 27).

Jacob's flight

After deceiving his father and his brother, Jacob fled to Haran, where he worked for his uncle Laban. On his way he stopped at Bethel, where he dreamed of a ladder leading to heaven.

While in Haran, Jacob married Laban's daughters Leah and Rachel, eventually returning to Canaan years later with his wives, children, servants, flocks and herds.

Jacob, or 'Israel' as he was now called, now settled in Canaan and became the father of the Israelites (Genesis 28–33).

Joseph

When Jacob sent his favourite son, Joseph, to visit his other sons, they sold him to passing Midianite traders, who in turn sold him as a slave in Egypt. But Joseph rose to become governor of Egypt and when famine came to Canaan, he brought his family to settle in Egypt (Genesis 42–46).

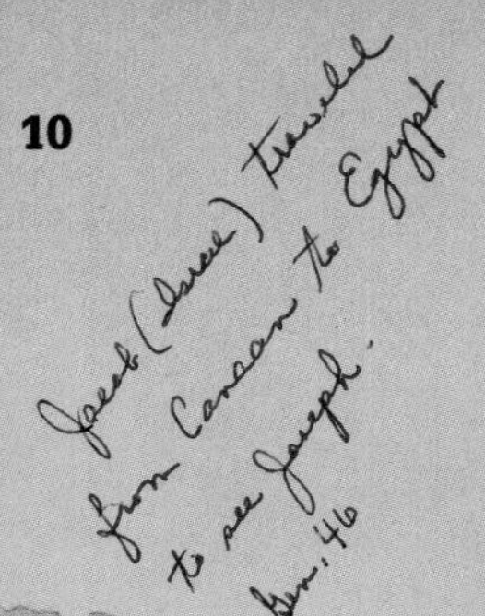
Jacob (Israel) traveled
from Canaan to Egypt
to see Joseph.
Gen. 46

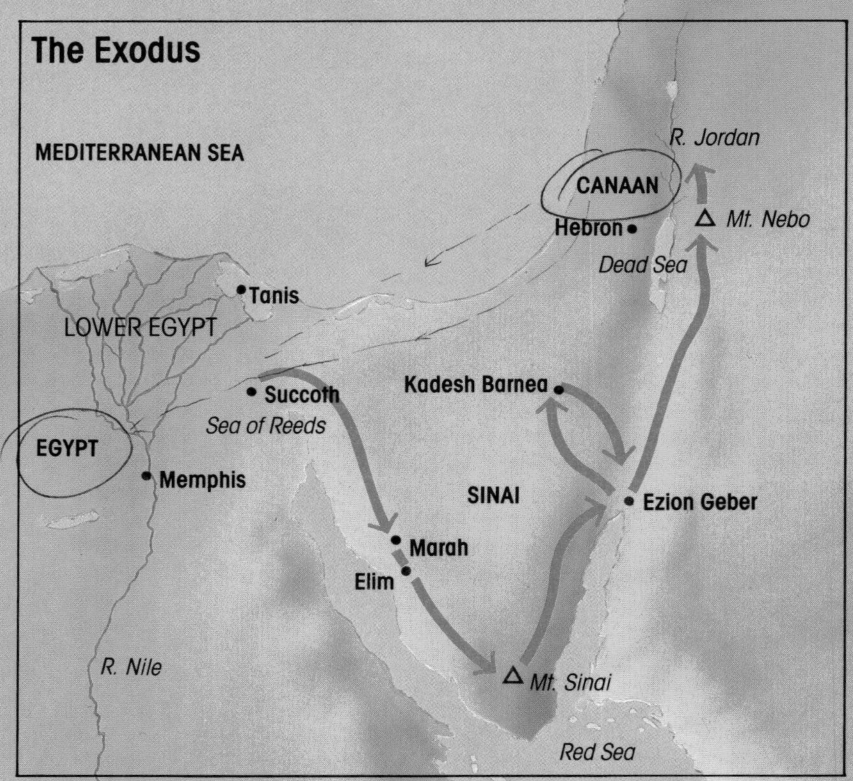
The Exodus
MEDITERRANEAN SEA
R. Jordan
CANAAN
Hebron
Mt. Nebo
Dead Sea
Tanis
LOWER EGYPT
Succoth
Sea of Reeds
Kadesh Barnea
EGYPT
Memphis
SINAI
Ezion Geber
Marah
Elim
R. Nile
Mt. Sinai
Red Sea

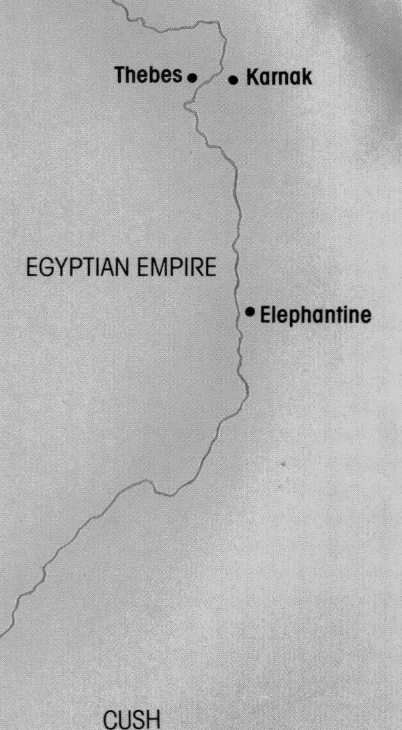
Thebes
Karnak
EGYPTIAN EMPIRE
Elephantine
CUSH

The Exodus

Jacob's sons settled in Egypt, in the eastern part of the delta of the river Nile, in the 'land of Goshen'.

At first they increased and prospered. But, after many years, a pharaoh rose to power who knew nothing about Joseph and his help to Egypt. This pharaoh, and his successor Rameses II (1299–1232), enslaved the Hebrew people.

Rameses wanted to build a great stronghold and to restore the city of Tanis as his capital city, so he set the Hebrews to work building and labouring.

Moses, a Hebrew who was brought up as a royal prince, and was therefore wealthy and educated, was chosen by God to lead his people out of Egypt.

Let my people go!

With his brother, Aaron, at his side, Moses appeared before Rameses to demand that he free the Hebrews. Pharaoh refused, even after a succession of terrible plagues; but he eventually relented and allowed them to leave.

After a hurried meal, later commemorated in the Passover, the Hebrews left Egypt. Moses led his people southeast to the Bitter Lakes (or Sea of Reeds), where they camped the first night.

Meanwhile Rameses changed his mind again and set out in pursuit. The Israelites escaped across the Sea of Reeds on dry land, but the pursuing Egyptians were drowned when the waters returned.

In the desert

The Israelites marched on. They came first to Marah, where they found the water too bitter to drink. Then they came to the oasis of Elim. While they were in the desert, God provided his people with quails and manna to eat.

After three months the Hebrew people arrived at Mount Sinai, where Moses received the Law from God, in the form of the Ten Commandments. On Mount Sinai God made a solemn agreement with his people.

The Hebrews stayed at Sinai for about a year before moving north toward the Promised Land (Exodus, Numbers).

Ancient Egyptian model of a sailing boat.

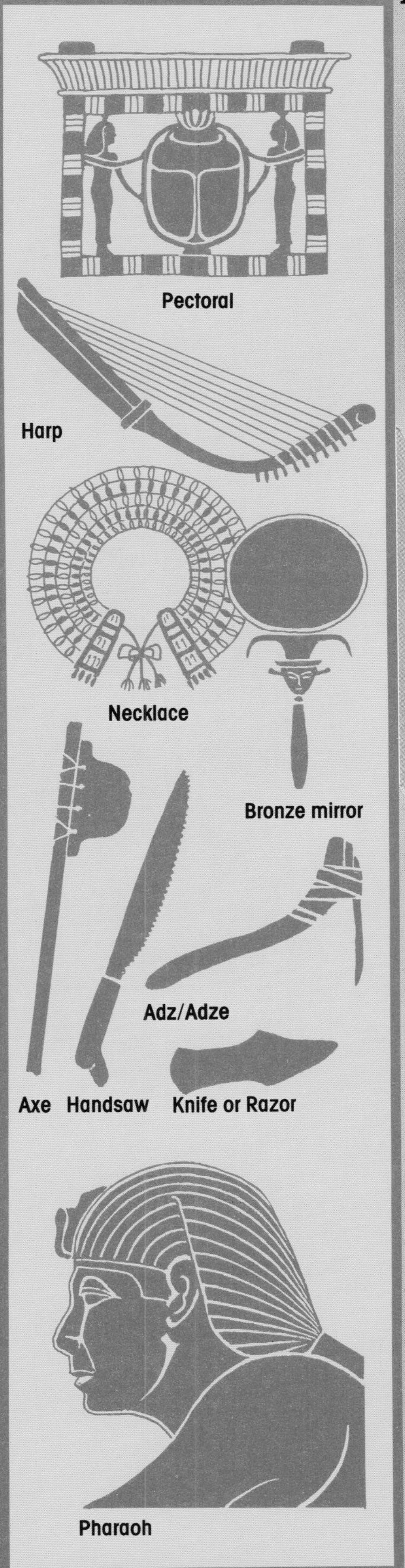

The Land

Although Palestine is not large, it contains a surprising variety of scenery and types of country.

The land can be divided into four major areas, all running roughly north-south. These four areas are: the coastlands, the central highlands, the Jordan Rift Valley, and the eastern plateau.

The Coastlands

A series of lowlands follow the Mediterranean coast, becoming wider toward the south. North of Mount Carmel is the Plain of Asher, reaching almost as far as the ancient Phoenician ports of Tyre and Sidon. Ptolemais (modern Akko) was the main port in Old Testament times.

South of Carmel is the Plain of Sharon, sandy near the coast and, in Bible times, swampy inland. Joppa (modern Jaffa) was the main port.

Still farther south, the coastal plain widens into low hills and fertile valleys; in Old Testament times this was the land of the Philistines. The 'Way of the Sea', leading from Egypt via Carmel to Damascus, ran across the coastal plain.

The Central Highlands

This central area consists of chalk and limestone hills. To the north is Galilee, with its open hill-country bounded on the east by the Sea of Galilee.

South of Nazareth is the triangular Plain of Esdraelon, a fertile area and, from ancient times, an important route across the country. This plain is linked to the Jordan valley by the Valley of Jezreel, where Saul and Jonathan fought their last battle.

South of Esdraelon the hills become more and more continuous, stretching towards Beersheba, on the edge of the Negev desert. East of Jerusalem lies the dry Judean Wilderness.

The Jordan Rift Valley

Part of a very long split in the earth's crust, this valley stretches from Dan in the north through the Plain of Huleh, the Sea of Galilee, and the Dead Sea toward the Gulf of Aqaba in the south. In places the surrounding hills drop very steeply to the valley. The Dead Sea is the lowest place on the earth's surface.

The Eastern Plateau

East of the Jordan valley lie limestone and sandstone highlands. Bashan, in the north, is quite fertile, as is the hilly area of Gilead. Edom, in the south, is barren and poor. Towards the south and east, the land becomes true desert.

Climate

Most of Palestine has what is called a Mediterranean climate – mid-way between temperate and tropical. Winters are mild and wet, summers dry and hot. In summmer, when there is usually no rain, scorching winds can blow from the deserts. But the wide seasonal differences mean that while snow still lies on the peak of Mount Hermon, tropical fruits are ripening in the plains. There is almost no rain in the desert to the south.

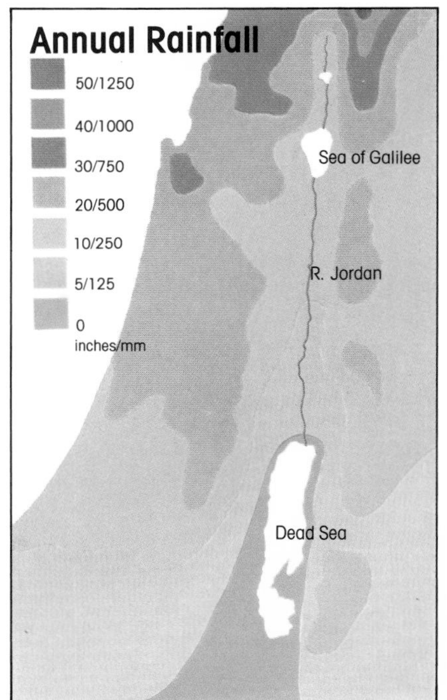

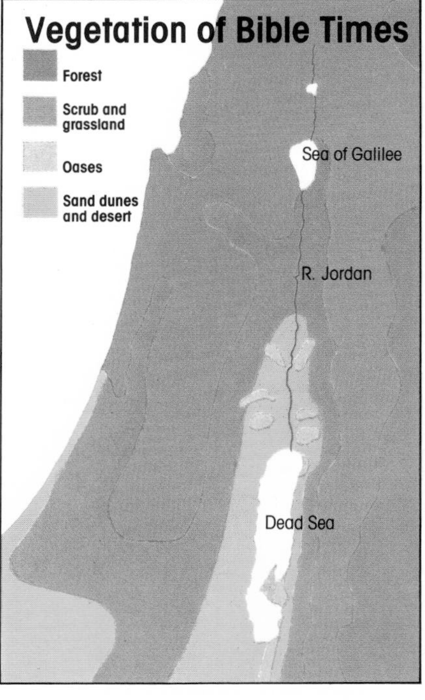

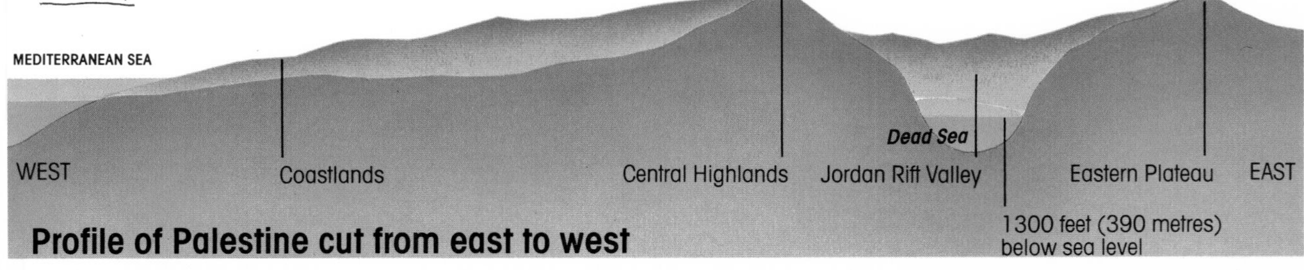

Profile of Palestine cut from east to west

Mt. Hermon
Dan
Tyre
PLAIN OF HULEH
BASHAN
GALILEE
Ptolemais
PLAIN OF ASHER
Sea of Galilee
Mt. Carmel
PLAIN OF ESDRAELON
MEDITERRANEAN SEA
GILEAD
VALLEY OF JEZREEL
EASTERN PLATEAU
Mt. Gilboa
JORDAN RIFT VALLEY
PLAIN OF SHARON
R. Jabbok
Joppa
R. Jordan
CENTRAL HIGHLANDS
Mt. Nebo
COASTAL PLAIN
Jerusalem
JUDEAN WILDERNESS
JUDEAN HILLS
SHEPHELAH
DESERT
Dead Sea
Beer-sheba
Scale:
0 10 20 30 Miles
0 10 20 30 40 Km
EDOM

Conquest

When the Israelites arrived at Transjordan, the land east of the Jordan valley, they were very close to Canaan. Some were happy to stay there, rather than try to enter the Promised Land.

Moses had now reached the end of his life. He knew he would never enter the Promised Land. He stood on the summit of Mount Nebo and looked out across the Jordan valley to the mountains of Canaan, stretching from Beersheba in the south to Mount Hermon in the far north.

After forty years' wandering in the desert, the Israelites were finally ready to enter the Promised Land.

Camped at Abel-Shittim, east of the Jordan, the Israelites had first to take the stronghold of Jericho to enter Canaan. Joshua, their new leader, sent scouts to spy out the land. With their reports to help him, he led the people across the river Jordan and camped at Gilgal.

Taking Jericho

From Gilgal, the Israelites attacked Jericho; God destroyed its walls, giving the Israelites a toehold in the Promised Land (Joshua 2–6).

The Israelites now had a route into Canaan; but the central highlands were still protected by the strategic city-fortress of Ai. After the first attack on Ai failed, because of the sin of one man, Joshua planned a further assault.

Ambush at Ai

Joshua set an ambush west of Ai under cover of night. Next morning he led out the main Israelite army in front of the city. When the king of Ai left his city to attack Joshua, the Israelites pretended to retreat, and the men of Ai pursued them, leaving their city unprotected. The Israelite ambush party entered the city, set fire to it, and rejoined the main army, routing the forces of Ai (Joshua 8).

Neighbouring cities were greatly impressed by the military power of the Israelites, and the men of Gibeon tricked Joshua into making a treaty with them. Later, in a surprise attack, Joshua defeated five Amorite kings at the battle of Gibeon (Joshua 9, 10).

Dividing the land

Joshua followed up these striking victories with military campaigns, first in the south, then in the north. The conquest and settlement of Canaan by the Israelites was under way; but many cities and territories still remained in enemy hands (Joshua 10, 11).

Now that the Israelites had entered the land, they divided it between the twelve tribes. But because the conquest was not yet complete, many tribes had difficulty settling the area allocated to them (Joshua 13–21).

Excavations at ancient Jericho.

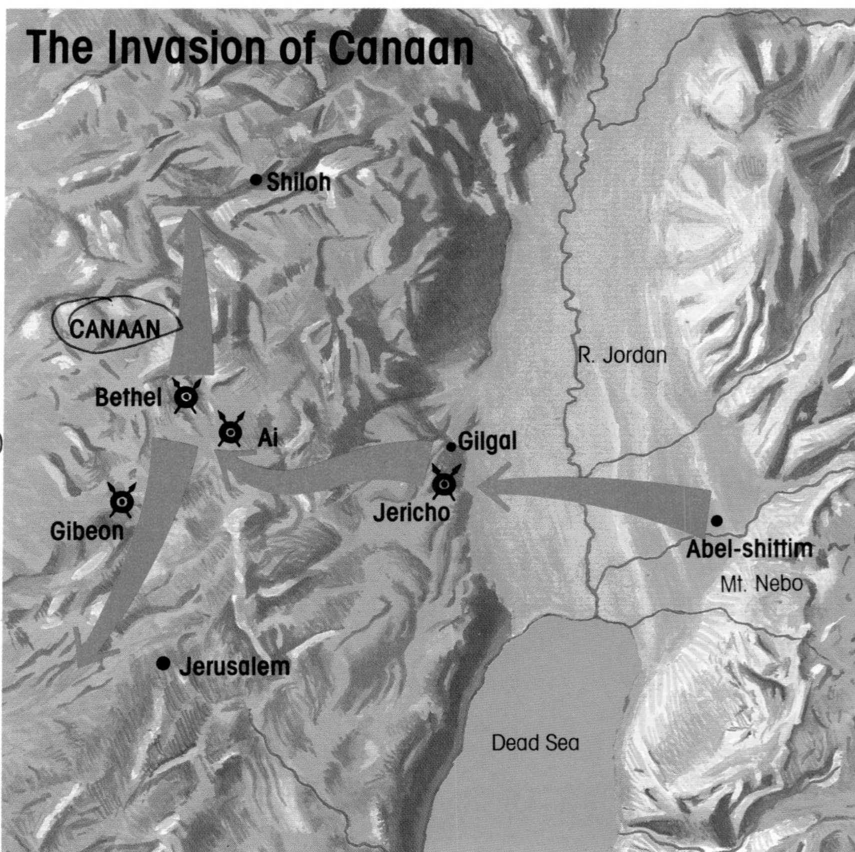

Canaan divided between the Twelve Tribes

Taking the Land

As we have seen, although the Israelites, led by Joshua, had entered Canaan, they had failed to complete the conquest. They were surrounded by hostile people worshipping foreign gods. They were frequently defeated and came under the rule of hostile peoples. Time after time one of the leaders of Israel called judges helped defeat the enemy and free the Israelites.

Deborah and Barak

Canaanites still held the fertile and strategic Plain of Esdraelon (or Jezreel). They had iron chariots and armed horsemen, which could beat the Israelite infantry on flat ground. Since the Canaanites held the plain, the Israelite tribes living in the north – Naphtali, Zebulun, and Issachar – became cut off from the southern tribes.

The Israelite prophetess Deborah raised a large army, persuaded Barak to lead it, and launched an attack on the Canaanites from the summit of Mount Tabor. A fierce thunder-storm flooded the valley, and the chariots of the Canaanites, who

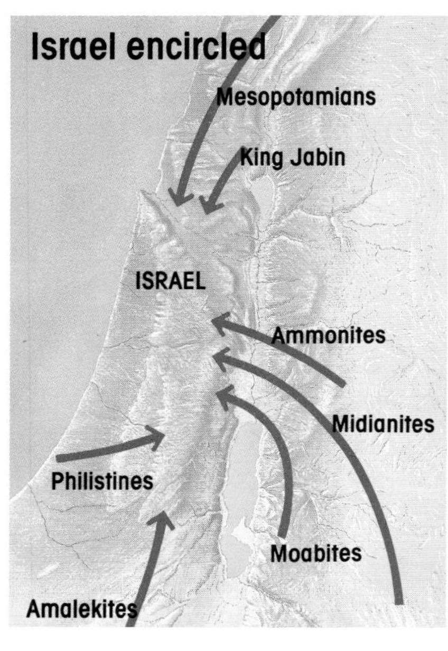

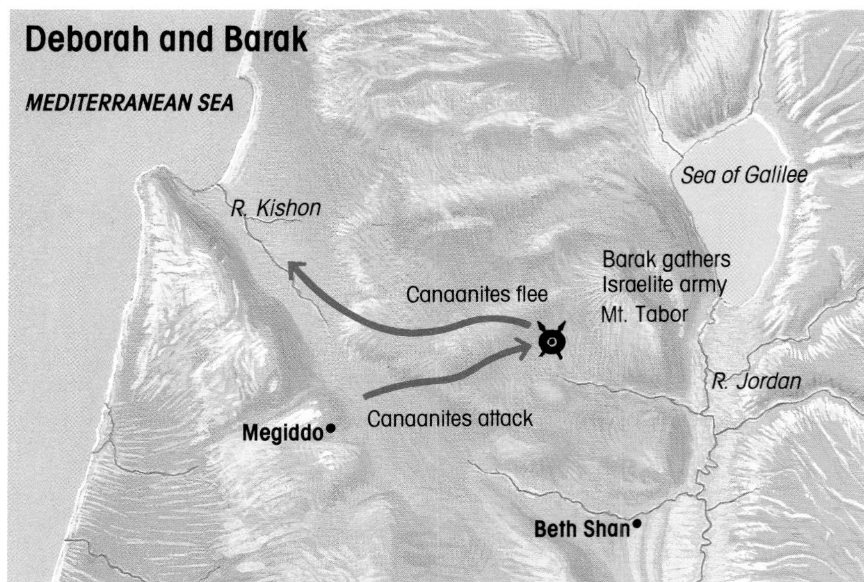

Philistine warriors.

were commanded by Sisera, stuck in the mud. By this victory Israel captured the Canaanite strongholds of Megiddo and Taanach (Judges 4, 5).

Gideon and the Midianites
When they settled in the Promised Land, the Israelites made great changes in their way of life. From being wandering shepherds, they now became a nation of farmers and craftsmen.

The Israelites also faced attack from wandering invaders, such as the Midianites, who entered the central highlands from east of the river Jordan.

When the Midianite army camped in the Jezreel valley, the Israelite leader Gideon called together an army to oppose them. He narrowed down his force to 300 men and led a surprise night attack, using trumpets and torches to give the impression of a much larger army. The Midianites fled in panic and were routed by the pursuing Israelites (Judges 6, 7).

The Philistines capture the Ark
Some years later the Philistines inflicted a heavy defeat on the Israelites at the battle of Aphek. When Israel fought the Philistines again at Ebenezer, they took the Ark of God, containing the tablets of the Law, into battle with them in the hope it would help them. But the Philistines won again and carried off the Ark as a prize. The Philistines first took the Ark to Ashdod, placing it in the temple of their god Dagon. But when the statue of Dagon fell and plague broke out, they sent the Ark to Gath, then to Ekron, and finally back to Israel. The Ark remained at Kiriath Jearim, in the Judean hills, for twenty years, until King David took it to his new capital city, Jerusalem (1 Samuel 4–7).

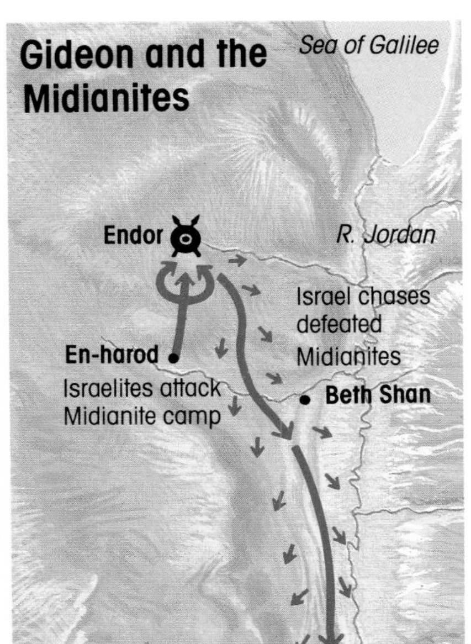

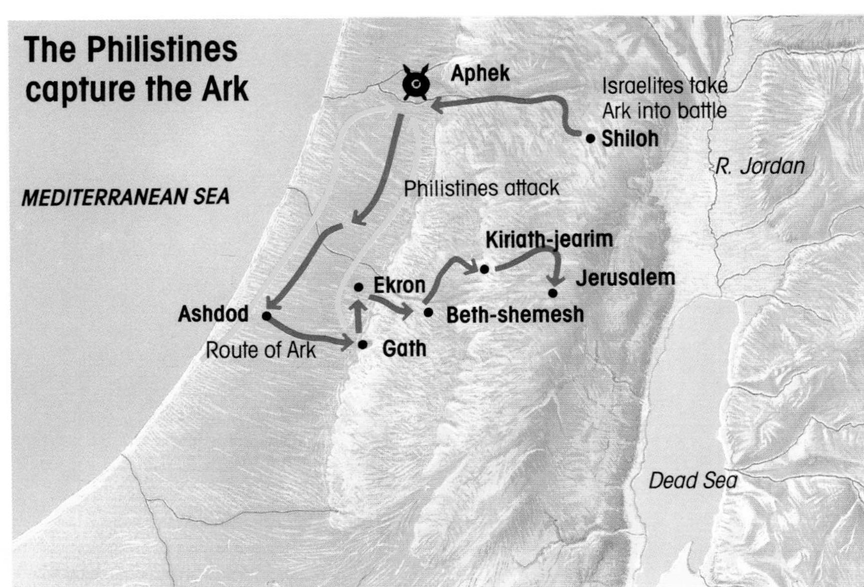

Israelite warriors.

The Kingdom of Saul and David

The prophet Samuel

One of the last of the Judges was Samuel, a prophet who travelled the country settling disputes. In 1050 BC he anointed Saul, the son of Kish, as king over all the tribes of Israel (1 Samuel 10).

For many years King Saul waged war, not only on the Philistines but also on other hostile neighbours.

Saul's jealousy

But when a young hero called David became popular with the people, Saul grew jealous. Finally David had to flee Saul's court, first seeking refuge with the Philistine king of Gath, then hiding in a cave at Adullam, in the Judean Wilderness, and finally retreating with his family to Moab, on the east side of the Dead Sea. When David returned to Judah, he was still pursued and had to go into exile in Ziklag in Gath (1 Samuel 16–26).

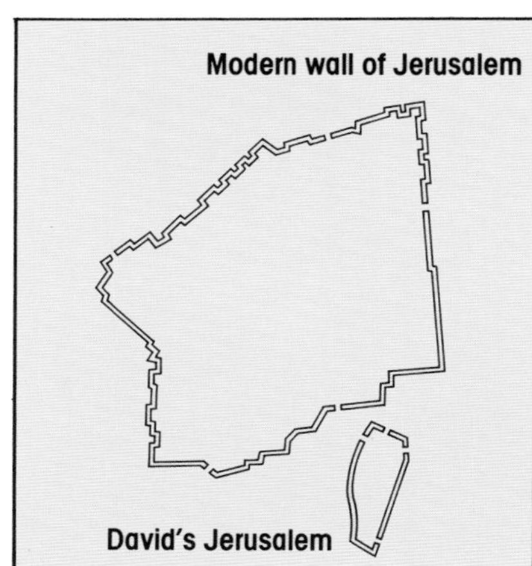

King David

As soon as he heard that Saul had been killed at the Battle of Gilboa, David went to Hebron, where he was anointed king of Judah, the southern part of the country. After two years' civil war, northern Israel also decided to recognize David as king; he now ruled the united nation.

David realized that it was important to set up a new capital city in the middle of his kingdom. He decided it should be at Jerusalem, which was still a Canaanite stronghold. After taking the city by entering via a water tunnel, David built his palace here and brought the Ark here.

David now launched a series of campaigns against the Philistines. He drove them back and captured the cities of Gath and Ziklag. He then set about further wars of conquest, defeating the Moabites, the Edomites, the Ammonites, and the Syrians, and greatly increased the boundaries of the kingdom (2 Samuel).

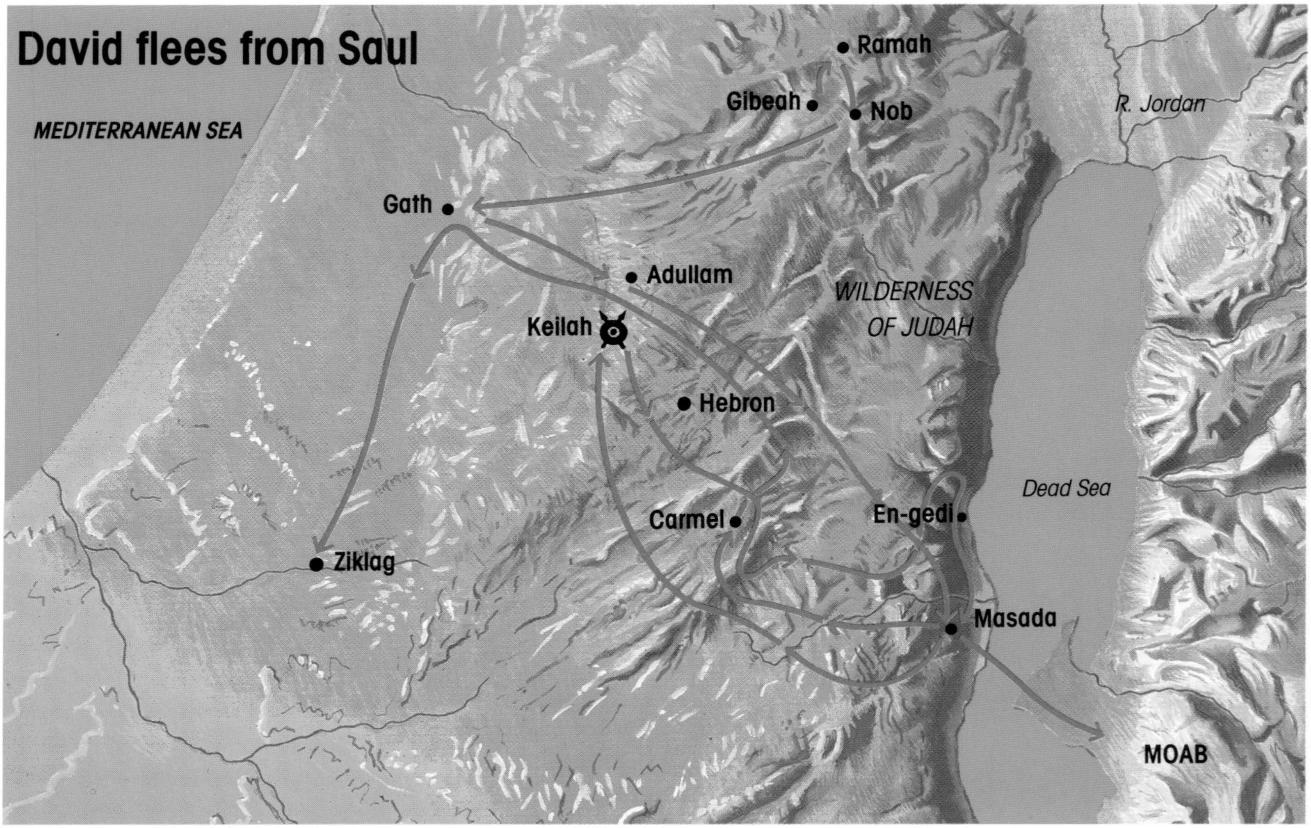

SIDONIANS
Tyre
Dan
SYRIA
Sea of Galilee
MEDITERRANEAN SEA
Megiddo
Beth Shan
Ramoth-gilead
ISRAEL
Shechem
Joppa
AMMON
Bethel
R. Jordan
Ashdod
Ashkelon
JUDAH
Jerusalem
Bethlehem
PHILISTINES
Hebron
Gaza
Dead Sea
Ziklag
Beer-sheba
MOAB
Zoar
EDOM

Solomon's Empire

When King David died in 970 BC, his son Solomon took the throne.

Solomon was a great ruler. He divided the kingdom into twelve new administrative districts, cutting across the boundaries of the tribes, and introduced a system of forced labour.

Solomon strengthened the old Canaanite strongholds of Megiddo, Beth Shan, Taanach, and Dor, and raised a large force of chariots based at these sites. He built large furnaces to smelt iron and copper in the south at Ezion-geber near the Gulf of Aqaba.

Solomon the trader

King Solomon greatly increased the nation's trade. His ships sailed down the Red Sea from Ezion-geber, bringing back goods such as red sandalwood, precious stones, gold, silver, ivory, spices, monkeys, and peacocks from what are today Zanzibar and Yemen.

Solomon also imported horses from Kue (Cilicia) near the Taurus Mountains in Asia Minor (modern Turkey), and chariots from Egypt.

One of Solomon's most important alliances was with Hiram, the Phoenician king of Tyre. Solomon obtained from Hiram much of the cypress and cedarwood that he needed for his great building programme. He built great warehouses at Hazor, Megiddo, Beth-horon, Gezer, Baalath, and Tamar to store his imports and exports (1 Kings 9, 10).

Solomon's capital

Solomon enlarged the boundaries of Jerusalem to make a capital worthy of his prosperous kingdom. He filled in the valley between the City of David (Ophel) and the higher ground to its north, where he built the magnificent Temple (1 Kings 5).

Solomon's Temple

To construct the Temple, Solomon brought in architects and metalworkers from Phoenicia. He used cedar and cypress wood from Phoenicia in building it. Although David had not been permitted by God to build the Temple, he had

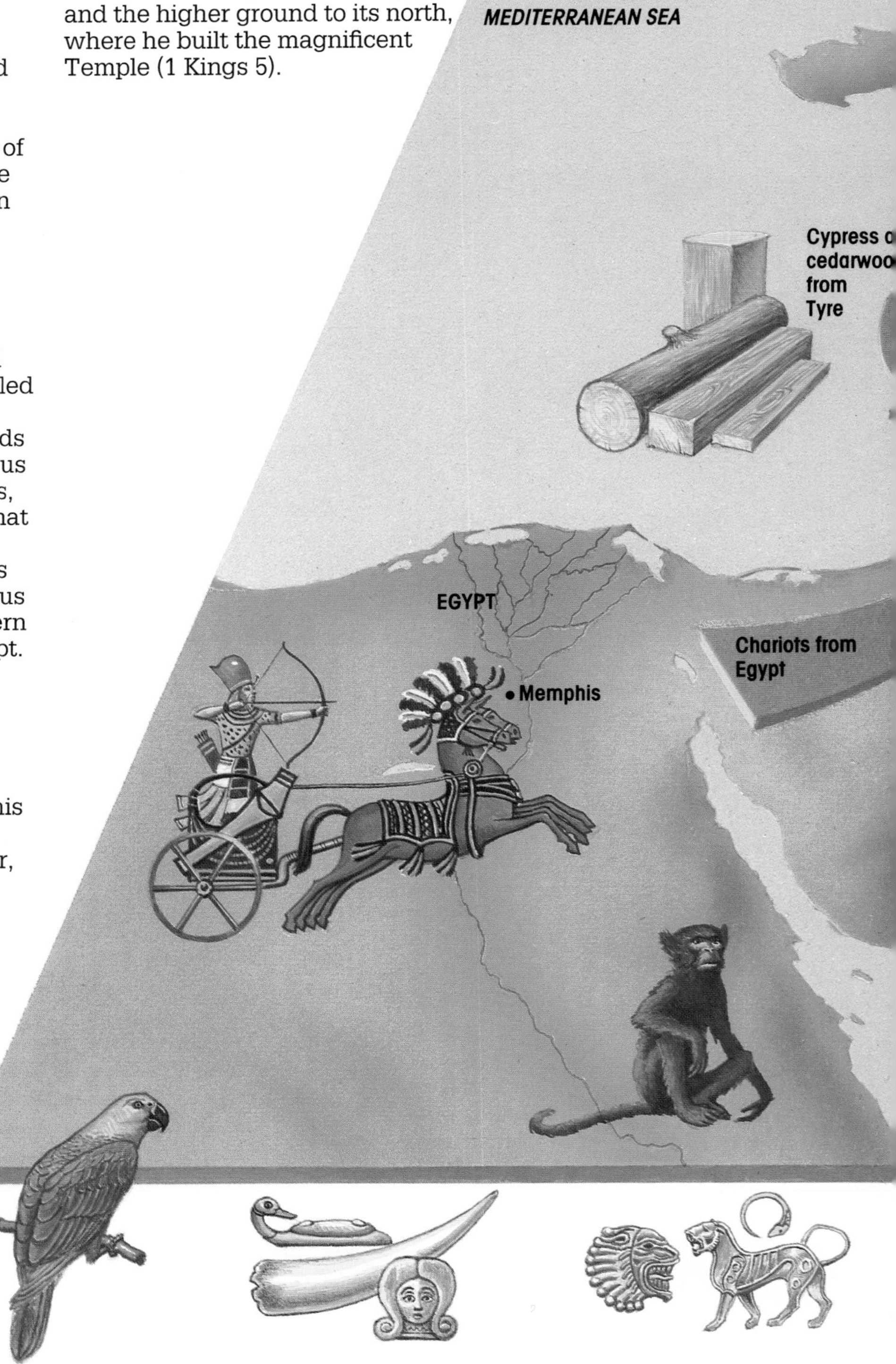

drawn up plans for it, which he handed on to his son Solomon. David had also gathered many of the building materials together – precious metals and other expensive items, collected in good-will offerings.

The Temple took a total of seven years in building; Solomon's palace thirteen years. Much bronze was used to ornament the Temple – for instance on the two great pillars at the entrance to the Temple, and on the furniture such as the altar and the bowl where the priests ritually washed. Much of the copper used for making this bronze was mined and smelted at Ezion-geber.

When the Temple was completed, a great service of dedication was held. The Ark of the Covenant was carried in by the priests and placed inside the Holiest Place. Solomon gave a blessing to all the people, and made a prayer of dedication. The first sacrifices were offered up, and then a great feast was held.

The Queen of Sheba

Many foreign visitors came to Jerusalem for trade and diplomacy, including the famous Queen of Sheba. Solomon gained the reputation of being one of the wisest men of his age. But, though he was wise, Solomon's love of power and display helped bankrupt the country, dividing it between the rich and the poor.

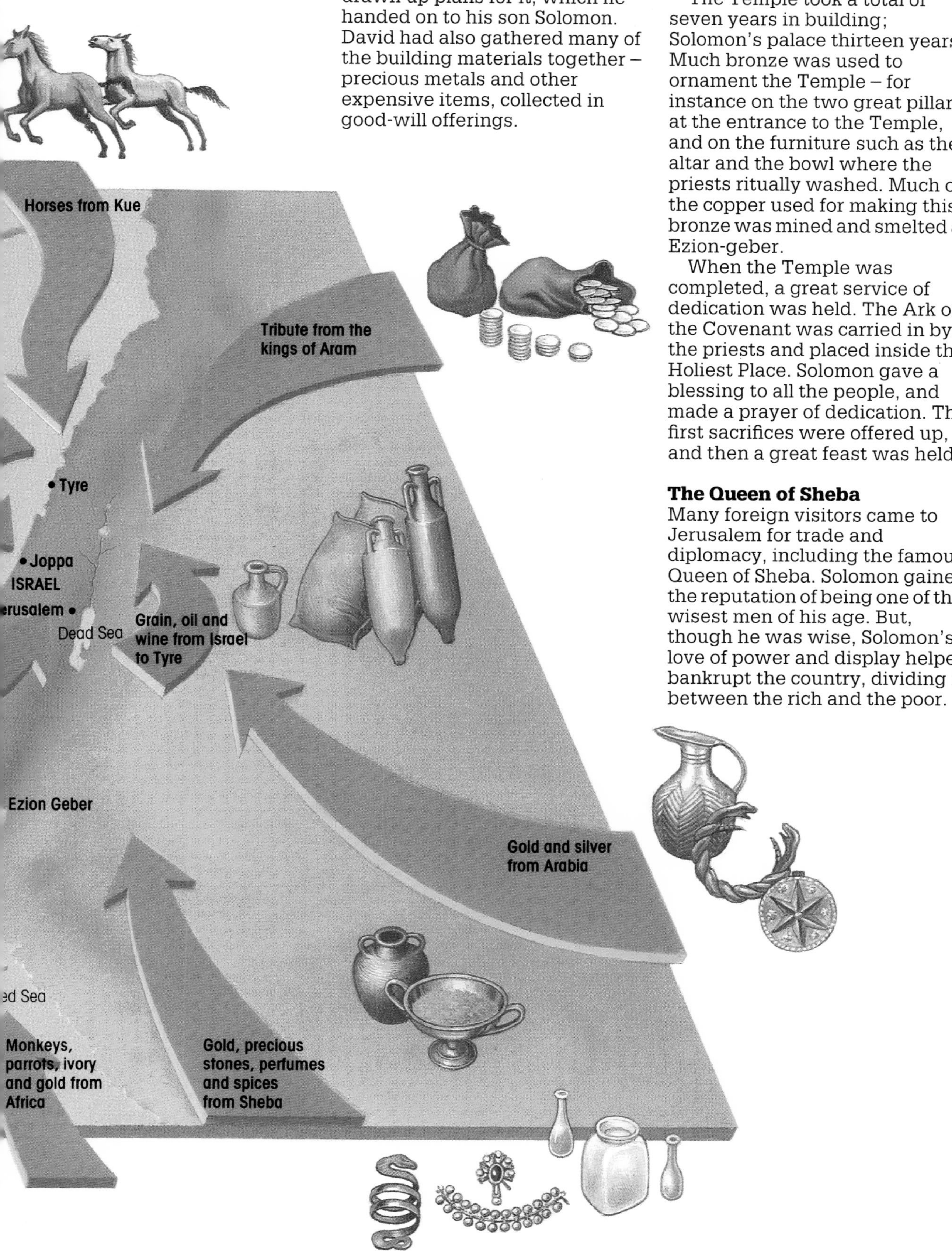

The Divided Kingdom

Until Solomon died, in 922 BC, the whole kingdom was known as Israel. But when Solomon's son Rehoboam became king in Jerusalem, Jeroboam led the northern tribes in rebellion (1 Kings 11, 12).

The kingdom divided into a southern part, Judah, and a northern part, Israel. There were many differences between the two. Differences in soil, climate, and geography; differences in history and culture.

Two kingdoms

Israel, in the north, had enough rain to grow grain, olives, and grapes; there were rich pastures with good cattle. Judah, in the south, was much drier and could not grow enough for its needs; it had to import some of its food.

Israel stood at the crossroads of the ancient world, in the middle of the Fertile Crescent, and was influenced by the Phoenicians and by the religion of other pagan neighbours.

Judah had more shepherds than farmers. It was not on any great crossroads, and its people stayed more faithful to God.

Judah

Rehoboam ruled over only Judah. He spent his reign trying unsuccessfully to recover Israel. The Egyptian pharaoh Shishak took the opportunity to invade and to capture Jerusalem.

Rehoboam's successors, Kings Abijah and Asa, continued the war with Israel, but King Jehoshaphat (873–848 BC) made peace with the north.

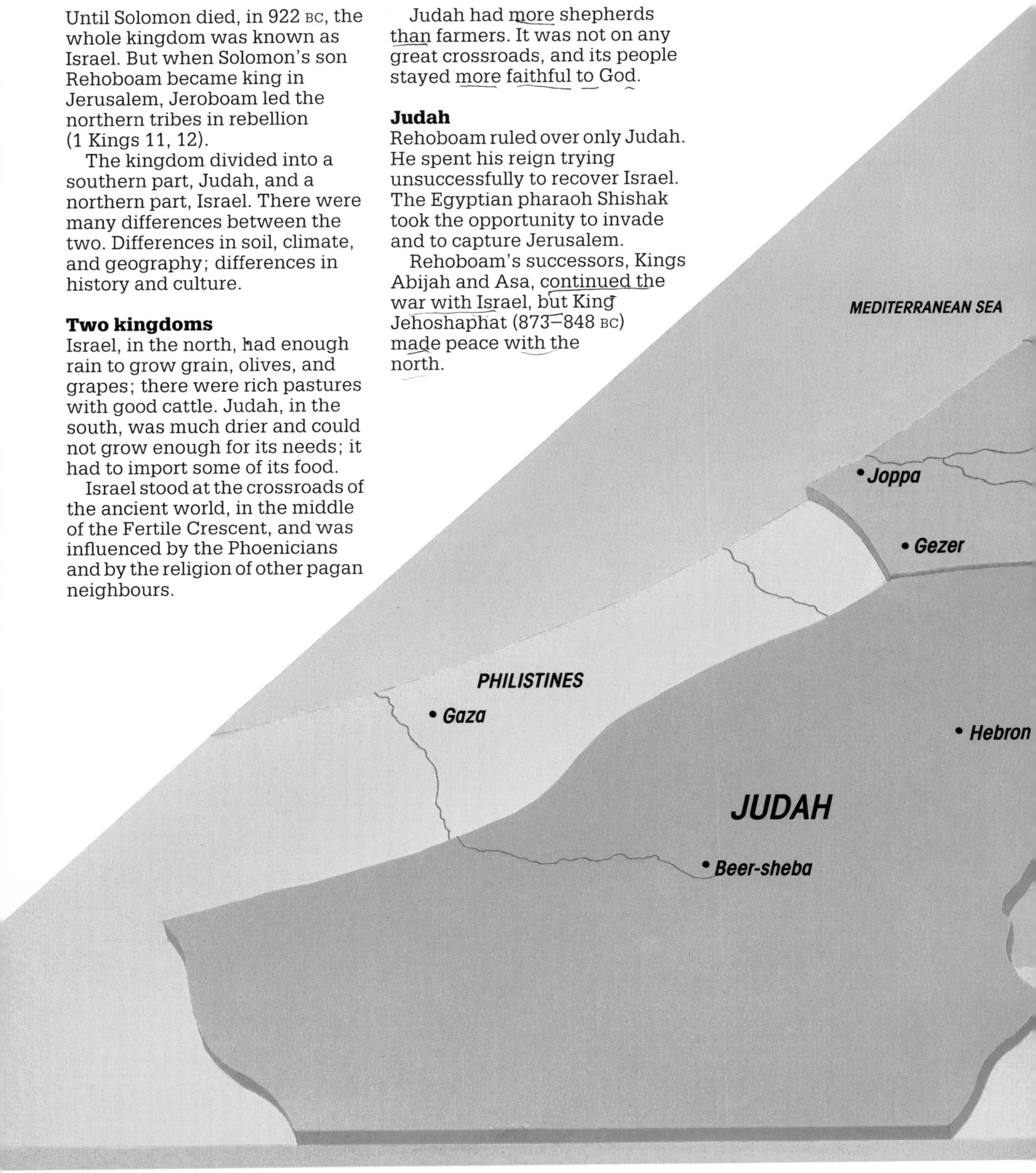

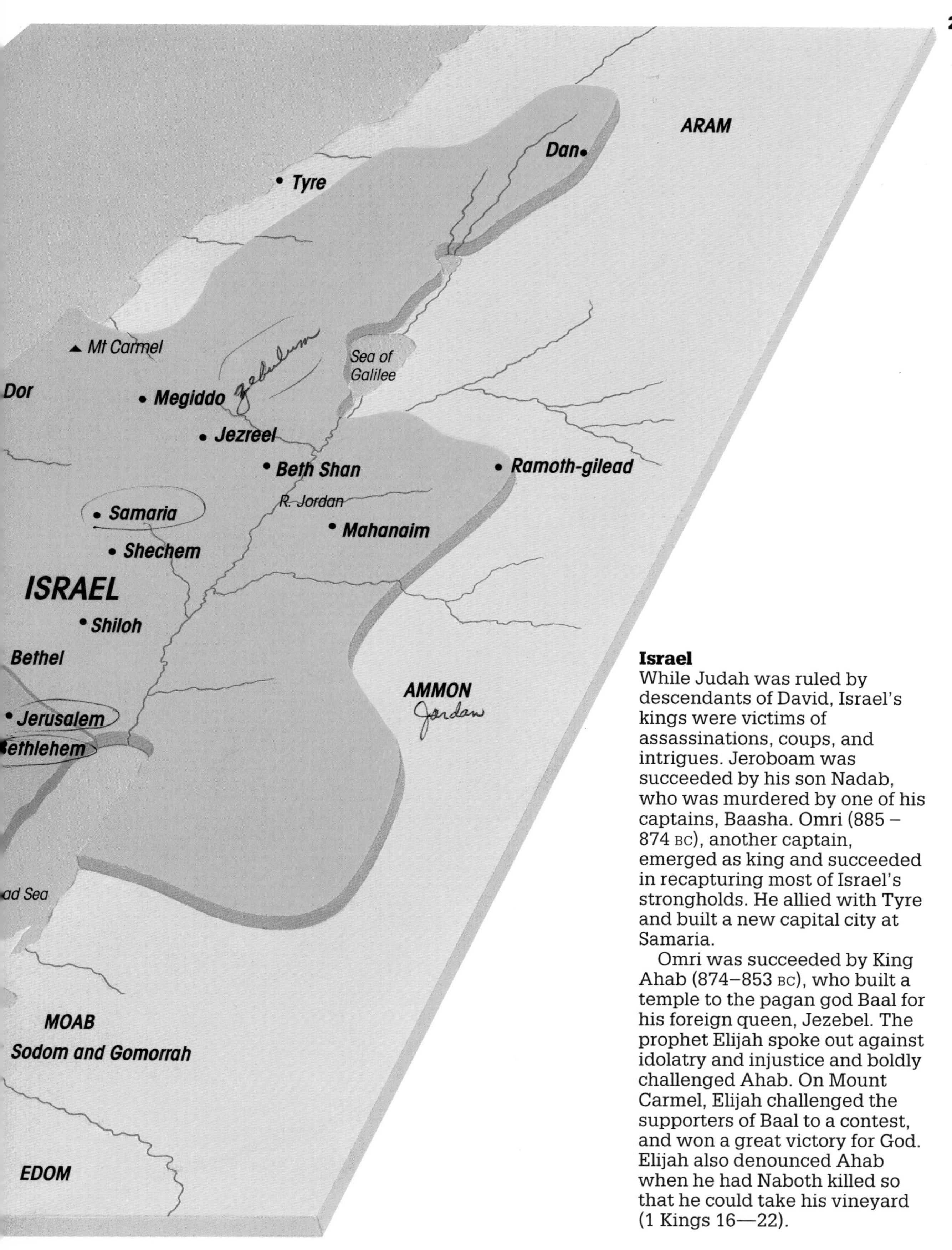

Israel
While Judah was ruled by descendants of David, Israel's kings were victims of assassinations, coups, and intrigues. Jeroboam was succeeded by his son Nadab, who was murdered by one of his captains, Baasha. Omri (885 – 874 BC), another captain, emerged as king and succeeded in recapturing most of Israel's strongholds. He allied with Tyre and built a new capital city at Samaria.

Omri was succeeded by King Ahab (874–853 BC), who built a temple to the pagan god Baal for his foreign queen, Jezebel. The prophet Elijah spoke out against idolatry and injustice and boldly challenged Ahab. On Mount Carmel, Elijah challenged the supporters of Baal to a contest, and won a great victory for God. Elijah also denounced Ahab when he had Naboth killed so that he could take his vineyard (1 Kings 16—22).

The Fall of Israel

The Assyrians carry off prisoners into exile; a relief from ancient Nineveh.

Around the time of King Ahab the terrible Assyrian Empire was rising in the east. The Assyrians were much feared for their cruelty in war – burning enemies alive and building pyramids of human skulls.

Ahab and Jehu

King Ahab, in alliance with King Ben-Hadad of Syria, defeated the Assyrians and temporarily halted their advance.

Ahab's son and successor, Joram, was killed by his general, Jehu, who then seized the throne. Supported by the prophet Elisha, King Jehu rid the nation of Baal-worship and massacred many Baal-worshippers. But he lost much of his territory to the Syrians.

Jehu was succeeded by his son Jehoahaz and by Jehoash, who recaptured some of the cities lost by Jehu.

There now followed a period of relative peace in the Fertile Crescent. Neither Assyria nor Egypt was strong enough to invade.

King Jeroboam II reigned for forty years, and restored some prosperity to his kingdom and increased trade.

But the prophet Amos, a poor shepherd from Tekoa in Judah, came to Bethel in Israel, denouncing injustice and warning that Israel would shortly be destroyed (Amos).

Assyria advances

By 745 BC the Assyrians, under Tiglath-Pileser III, were on the march. Their advance brought panic to Israel, and a man named Menahem took the throne. When the Assyrians moved south, Menahem managed to buy them off with a huge sum of gold.

Israel was in chaos. More assassinations followed, and the kingdom was without an ally. The prophet Hosea predicted the end of the kingdom of Israel. He called his nation 'a dove, silly and without sense, calling to Egypt, going to Assyria'.

Ruined wall at ancient Samaria.

The hills of northern Israel.

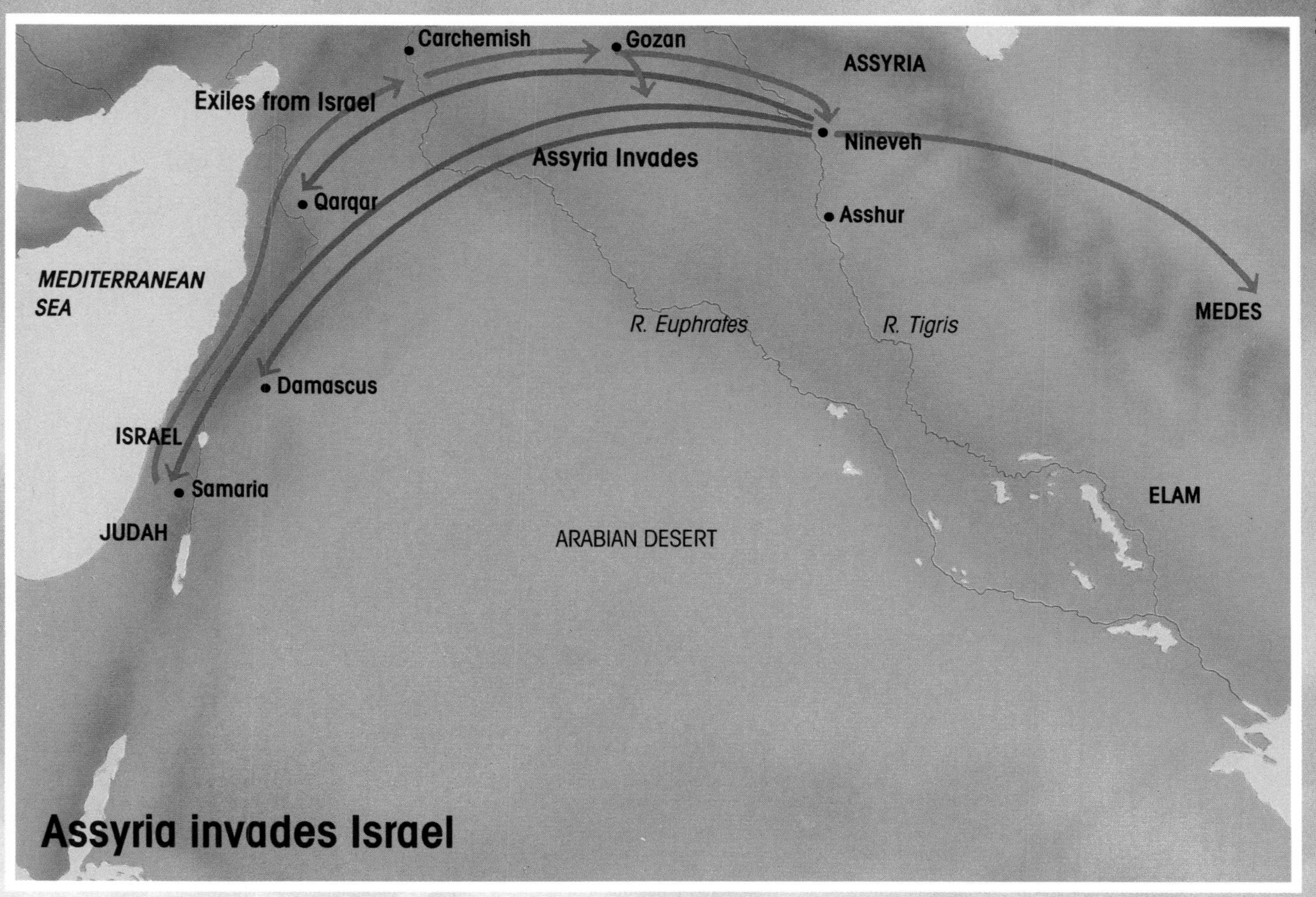

Into captivity

King Pekah of Israel made an alliance with King Rezin of Damascus. But in 732 BC Tiglath-Pileser captured Damascus after a two-year siege, also taking the Israelite territories of Galilee and Transjordan. He carried off the Israelites into captivity and replaced Pekah with a puppet king, Hoshea.

When Tiglath-Pileser died, King Hoshea of Israel tried to ally with Egypt against the new Assyrian emperor, Sargon II. But after a three-year siege, Sargon captured Samaria, the capital of Israel, in 722 BC and sent the entire population into exile in distant parts of his empire (2 Kings 17).

Hoshea was the last king of Israel. The Israelites, sometimes known as the 'ten lost tribes', disappeared completely from history.

The Fall of Judah

Athaliah, a daughter of King Ahab, married Jehoram, king of Judah. When her son Amaziah was killed, she seized the throne herself, until she was forcibly replaced by her young grandson, Joash (835 – 796 BC).

Judah, like Israel, was at risk from Assyria. The prophet Isaiah warned of the danger but promised that a 'remnant' would repent and remain.

Hezekiah rebels

After the fall of Israel, Judah remained independent, though King Ahaz had to pay a yearly tax to Assyria. Ahaz's son, King Hezekiah (716–687 BC), rebelled, but the Assyrian emperor Sennacherib put down his revolt, though he did not succeed in capturing Jerusalem (2 Kings 18, 19).

Prophets such as Micah continued to prophesy the destruction of Jerusalem and of the Temple.

Josiah, one of the few kings of Judah to please God, followed Hezekiah. When Nineveh, the Assyrian capital, fell to the Babylonians, Egypt invaded Judah. King Josiah (641–609 BC) was killed in battle against Neco of Egypt, and his son Jehoiakim took the throne.

Jerusalem falls

The Babylonians now defeated Egypt at the battle of Carchemish, and Nebuchadnezzar of Babylon marched on Jerusalem, capturing the city and marching the princes, priests, officers, and craftsmen of Judah into captivity in Babylon.

Zedekiah was left as puppet king. When, despite the warnings of the prophet Jeremiah, Zedekiah tried to rebel, Nebuchadnezzar besieged and captured Jerusalem in 586 BC, destroying the walls and palaces and burning the Temple. The entire population, except the very poorest, was taken into exile (2 Kings, Jeremiah).

The Return

Although the Israelites disappeared, the people of Judah stayed together. They were encouraged by the prophets Jeremiah and Ezekiel.

In 539 BC King Cyrus of Persia became the great ruler of the east, defeating first the Medes, then the Babylonians. He offered the Jews the opportunity to return to Judah; few seized the chance.

A handful of priests and their families went back to the ruins of Jerusalem, and eventually, under the leadership of Nehemiah, rebuilt the walls of the city. They also constructed a temple on a more modest scale than Solomon's (Nehemiah 1, 2).

The scribe Ezra helped restore the Jewish faith, reading publicly the five books of the Law (Ezra 1–7).

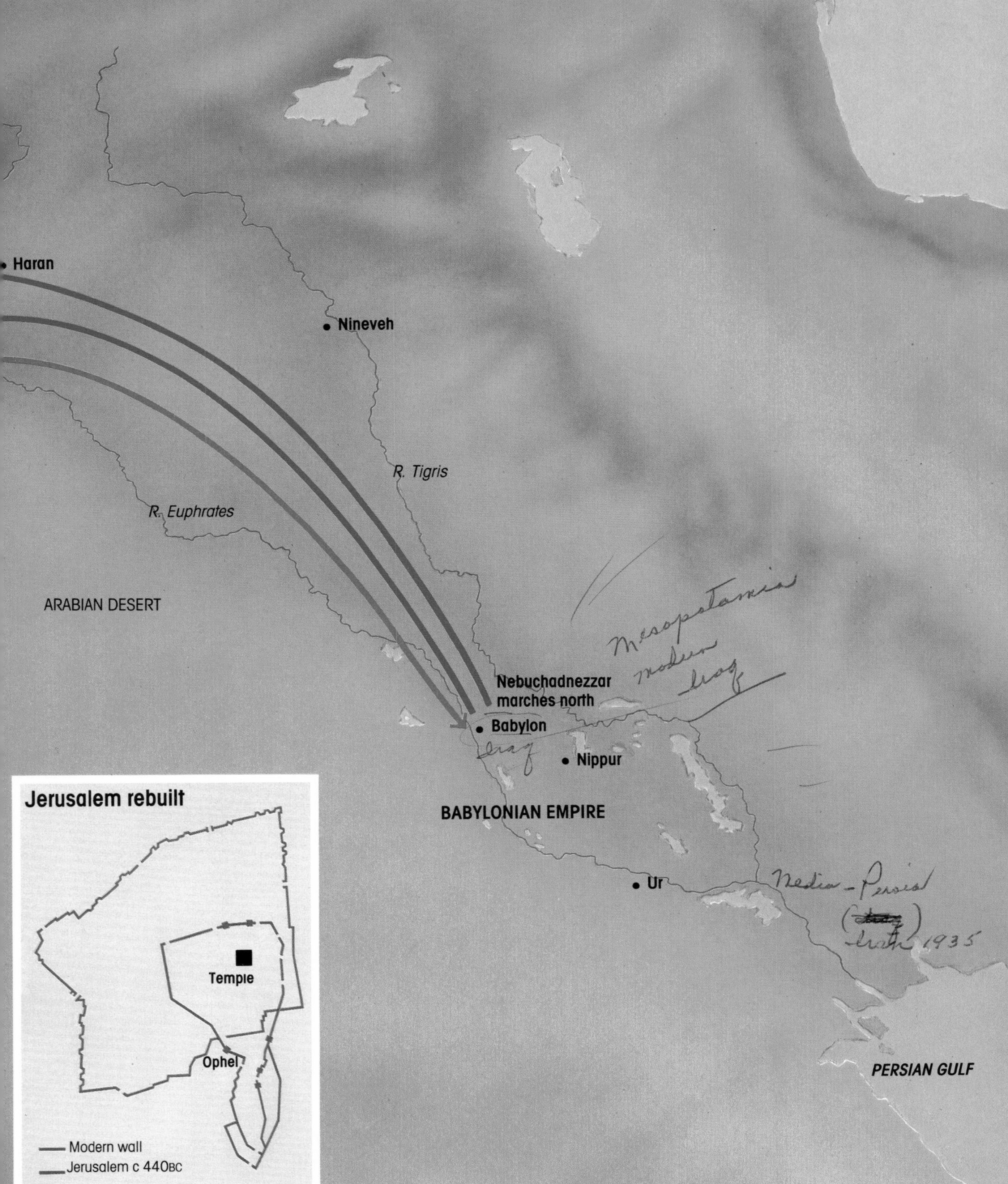
Haran
Nineveh
R. Tigris
R. Euphrates
ARABIAN DESERT
Nebuchadnezzar
marches north
Babylon
Nippur
BABYLONIAN EMPIRE
Ur
PERSIAN GULF
Jerusalem rebuilt
Temple
Ophel
Modern wall
Jerusalem c 440BC

Between the Testaments

After two hundred years, the Persian Empire began to weaken. A new conqueror came from Europe, Alexander of Macedon (336–323 BC). Aged only twenty-one, handsome, well-educated, and able, Alexander led his armies across what is modern Turkey and into Asia, capturing Damascus, Sidon, Tyre, and Jerusalem.

Alexander's conquests

Alexander went on to capture Egypt and founded the city of Alexandria. Defeating the Persian emperor, he captured the cities of Babylon, Susa, and Persepolis. Alexander reached as far as the borders of India before he died in Babylon at the age of thirty-three.

Upon his death, Alexander's generals fought over his empire. The Ptolemies now ruled Egypt; the Seleucids ruled Syria. The Seleucids won control of Palestine and brought Greek ('Hellenistic') thinking, dress, and ways of living to the Jews.

The Seleucids

A Seleucid ruler named Antiochus Epiphanes (175–163 BC) even tried to make the Jews worship Greek gods. But an old priest named Mattathias refused and, with his five sons, formed a resistance movement.

Judas 'the Hammer'

Led by Judas Maccabaeus 'the Hammer', Mattathias's son, the Jewish fighters drove Antiochus's army out of Jerusalem and purified the Temple.

Judas's brothers, Simon and Jonathan, won the independence of Palestine and founded a new dynasty, the Hasmoneans, who were both high priests and kings.

Although Simon and Jonathan were both killed, Simon's brother

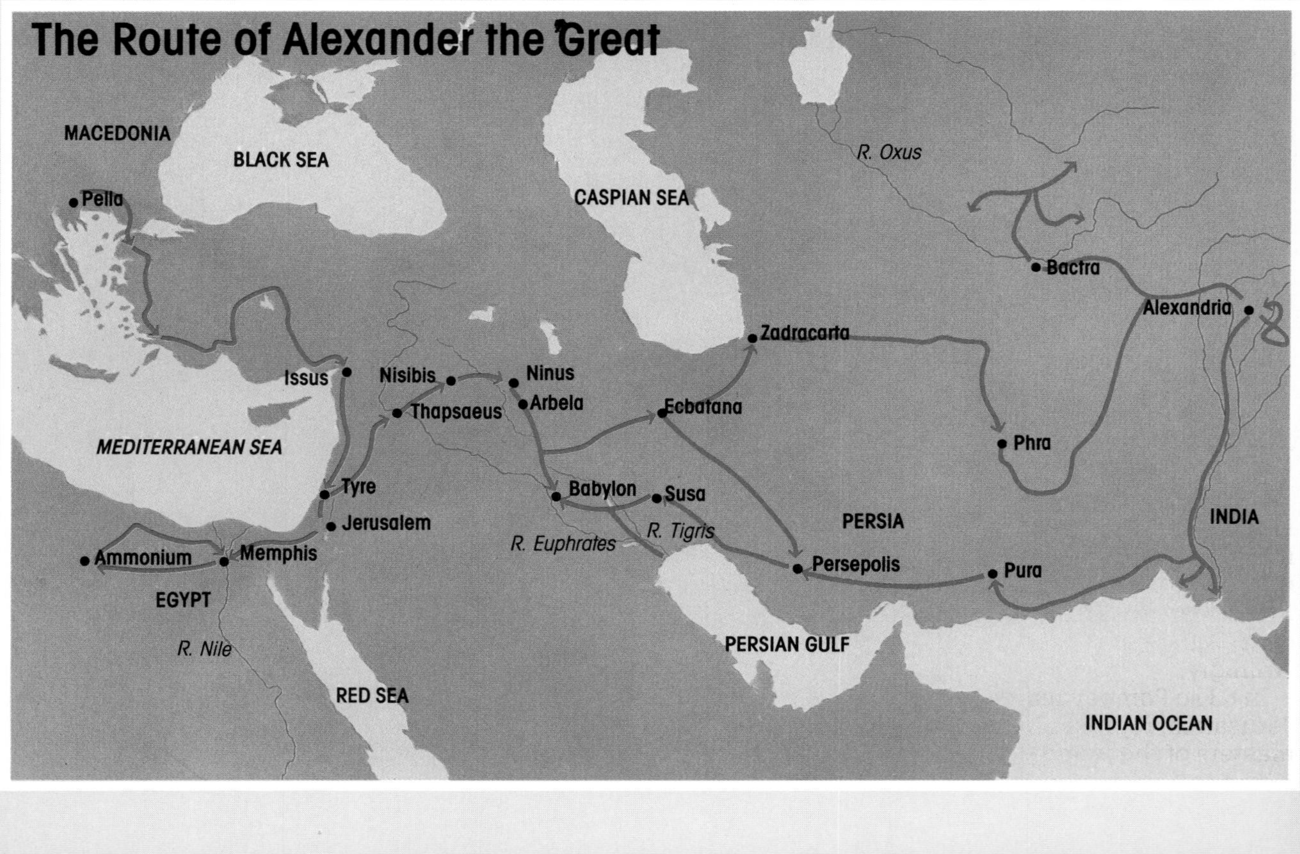

The Route of Alexander the Great

MACEDONIA
BLACK SEA
CASPIAN SEA
R. Oxus
Pella
Bactra
Alexandria
Zadracarta
Issus
Nisibis
Ninus
Arbela
Thapsaeus
Ecbatana
MEDITERRANEAN SEA
Phra
Tyre
Babylon
Susa
Jerusalem
PERSIA
INDIA
Ammonium
Memphis
R. Euphrates
R. Tigris
Persepolis
Pura
EGYPT
R. Nile
PERSIAN GULF
RED SEA
INDIAN OCEAN

Right: This tomb just outside Jerusalem was built in the Hellenistic style about 200 years before the birth of Christ.

Below: The so-called 'Tomb of Absalom', also Hellenistic in style.

Below right: Decorated Greek vase, showing a hero's shrine.

Opposite: Greek mosaic of Dionysus, god of wine.

John Hyrcanus reigned successfully for thirty years. He won control of Samaria and destroyed the rival temple of the Samaritans on Mount Gerizim.

When Hyrcanus's sons Aristobulus I and Alexander Jannaeus succeeded him, they further enlarged the kingdom. But many Jews felt that they were more interested in military conquest than in the worship of God.

Pompey enters Jerusalem

Eventually civil war broke out between Alexander Jannaeus's sons. Antipater, the governor of Edom, sided with one of them, Hyrcanus, who also appealed to the Roman general Pompey for help. Pompey responded willingly.

In 63 BC Pompey marched into Jerusalem, representing the new masters of the world – the Romans.

The New Testament World

The Roman Empire

The Romans, like the Greeks, came from Europe. Rome had begun as a city-state and republic but had formed colonies in many parts of the Mediterranean world.

Pompey came to the Middle East to win control of the area for Rome. When he entered the city of Jerusalem in 63 BC this brought to an end Palestine's independence.

Pompey immediately shocked the Jews by entering the Holiest Place in the Temple, where only the high priest was allowed only once a year.

Pompey made Hyrcanus II high priest, but Antipater was the real ruler. Hated by the Jews, Antipater was murdered in 43 BC.

Herod the Great

Rome named Antipater's son Herod new 'king of the Jews'. King Herod (37–4 BC) was a pagan and for this reason, and because he was the tool of the Romans, was hated by the Jews.

Herod attempted to be all things to all people. He built temples to his Roman master, Augustus, who was worshipped as a god. He built towns in the Greek style.

But Herod also paid his respects to the Jewish religion, rebuilding the Temple in Jerusalem on a monumental scale, with vast new terraces and porticos and rich decoration.

The Roman world

The first Roman emperor, Augustus (27 BC – AD 14), was a very capable administrator and ruler. He divided the empire into a number of subject states and kingdoms ruled by puppet kings or by Roman governors called 'procurators'.

Although Jesus was born in the reign of Augustus, his ministry, death and resurrection took place during the reign of his successor, Tiberius (AD 14–37). Paul's missionary journeys took place during the reigns of Claudius (AD 41–54) and the notorious Nero (AD 54-68). Nero was the emperor to whom Paul made his appeal.

Top: The theatre at Beth Shan, Roman Scythopolis.

Above: Ruins of the Forum, Rome, centre of Roman government.

Right: The Emperor Augustus.

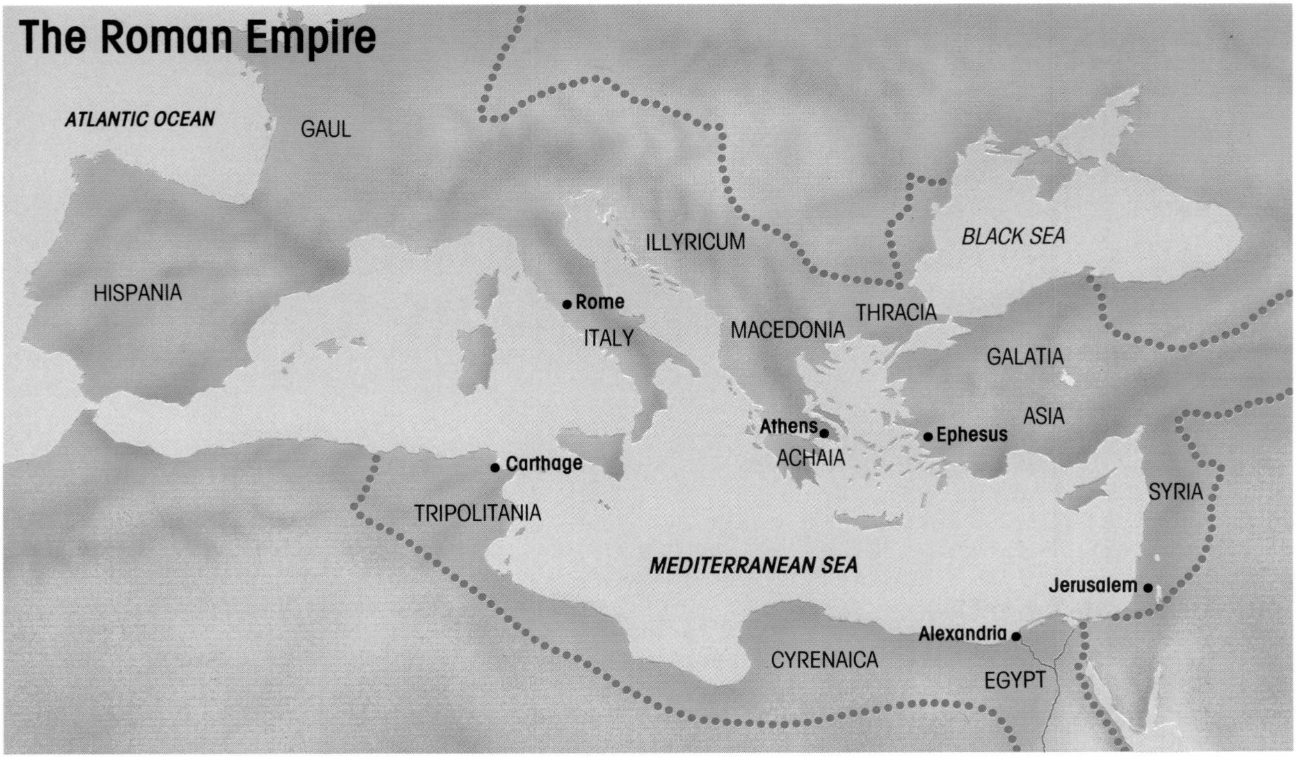

The Roman Empire

ATLANTIC OCEAN
GAUL
HISPANIA
ILLYRICUM
BLACK SEA
Rome
ITALY
MACEDONIA
THRACIA
GALATIA
ASIA
Athens
Ephesus
ACHAIA
Carthage
TRIPOLITANIA
SYRIA
MEDITERRANEAN SEA
Jerusalem
Alexandria
CYRENAICA
EGYPT

The Emperor Tiberius

The Roman aqueduct at the port of Caesarea.

The empire was linked together by a network of straight, hard-surfaced roads, which allowed trade to prosper and the Roman army to move swiftly to quell any disorder. During the height of the Roman Empire the roads and seaways were kept open and safe for travel.

The Roman army itself was highly efficient. Divided into legions of about 5,000 men, the soldiers were well-equipped and well-disciplined and could be relied on to keep order throughout the empire.

The Roman way of life

Roman culture was similar in many ways to the Greek culture introduced into Palestine after Alexander's campaign. The Romans built cities with features we now recognize as characteristic: baths, temples, aqueducts, market-places and the rest.

The Jews hated this pagan culture. From time to time they revolted against their Roman overlords but were crushed with ruthless efficiency. For instance, around the time of the birth of Jesus, a Roman general crucified 2,000 Jews after riots in Jerusalem.

New Testament Palestine

The Jews
The Jews hated the Roman occupying powers. But different Jewish groups reacted to the Romans in different ways.

The **Sadducees**, a wealthy group who were friends of the high priests, tended to collaborate with the Romans. They decided this was their best way of protecting their wealth and position.

The **Pharisees** and **scribes**, learned and religious Jews, did not collaborate. They drew aside from public affairs and devoted themselves to religious duties.

The **Essene** sect, and other religious extremists, withdrew almost completely from ordinary life. The Essenes, for instance, set up a monastery at Qumran on the barren shores of the Dead Sea, isolated from the Roman world. It was here that the famous Dead Sea Scrolls were discovered, in 1946.

Yet other Jewish extremists took up armed resistance. The **Zealots**, mainly from the hill country of Galilee, waged guerilla war on the Romans. They were led by a number of so-called 'messiahs', who were all in turn crushed by the Romans.

The ordinary people – the shepherds, peasants, and craftsmen, who also hated the Romans, were torn between the religious teachings of the Pharisees and the threats of the Zealots.

How Palestine was governed
When Herod the Great died in 4 BC, the Romans divided up his kingdom into three separate areas, each governed by one of his sons.

From 4 BC to AD 6 Herod's son **Archelaus** governed Judea, Samaria, and Idumea. After this the Romans ruled this area with governors, or procurators, who made their capital at Caesarea on the Mediterranean coast. Pontius Pilate is the best-known of these procurators.

Herod Antipas, another of Herod the Great's sons, ruled Galilee and Peraea. He built a new capital city on the Sea of Galilee and named it Tiberias in honour of the second Roman emperor. It was Herod Antipas who had John the Baptist beheaded. It was also Antipas to whom Pilate sent Jesus during his trial, since Jesus came from Galilee.

Herod's third son, **Philip,** ruled the areas of Ituraea and Trachonitis, northeast of Galilee. He made Caesarea Philippi his capital.

The Decapolis, a league of ten cities, lay south of Philip's territory. Jesus visited towns there at least twice.

The Dead Sea Scrolls were discovered in these caves near Qumran.

Coin picturing the goddess Hygeia, symbol of the hot springs at Tiberias.

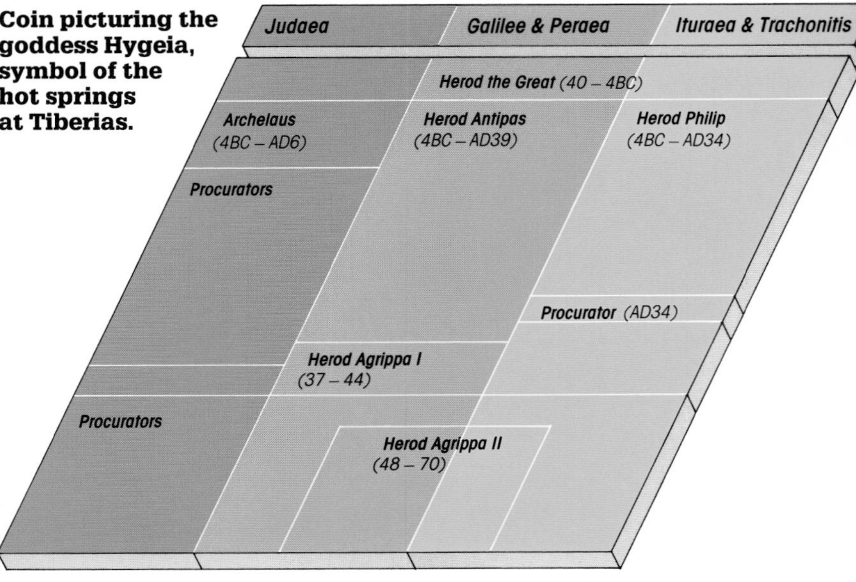

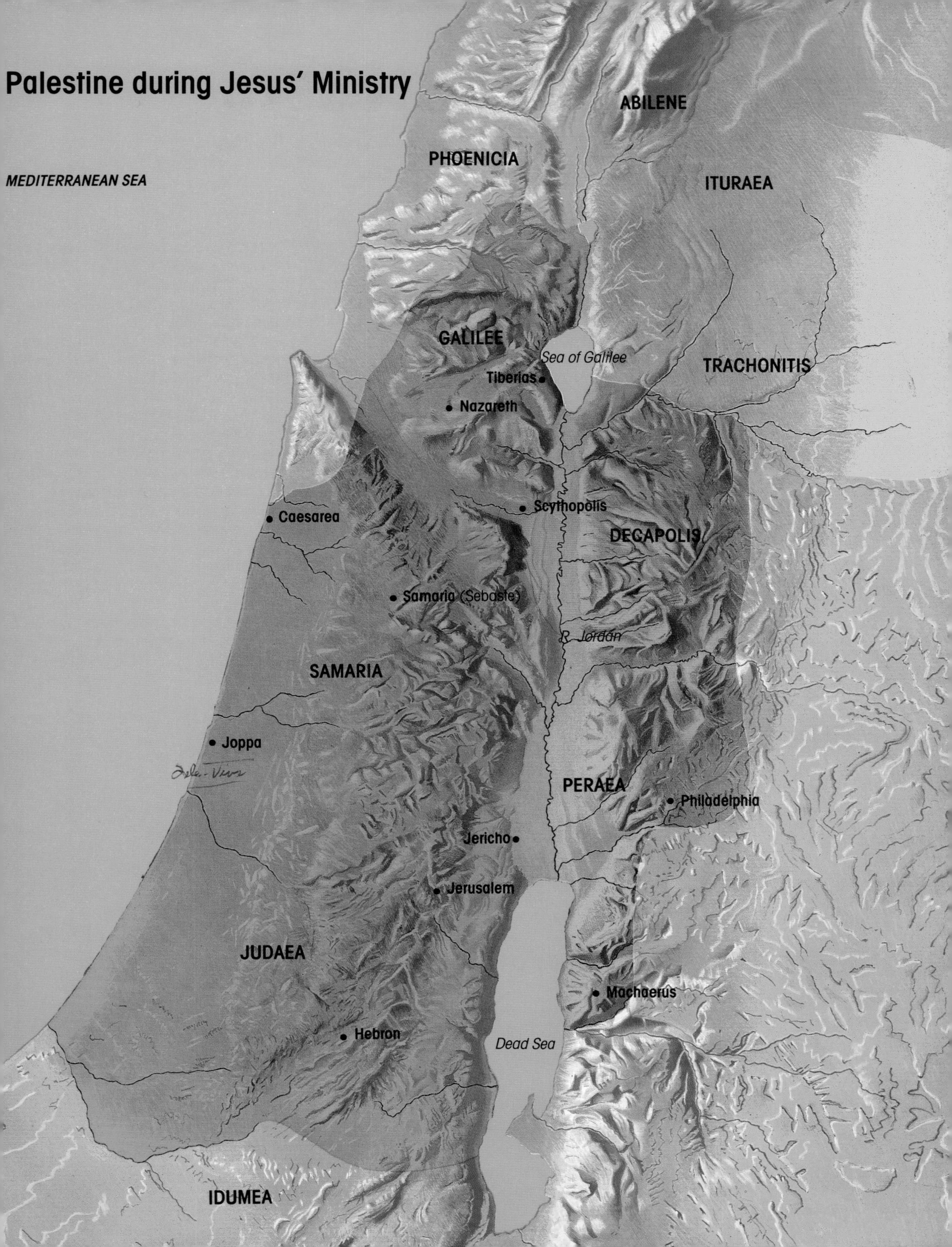
Palestine during Jesus' Ministry
MEDITERRANEAN SEA
PHOENICIA
ABILENE
ITURAEA
GALILEE
Sea of Galilee
TRACHONITIS
Tiberias
Nazareth
Scythopolis
Caesarea
DECAPOLIS
Samaria (Sebaste)
R. Jordan
SAMARIA
Joppa
PERAEA
Philadelphia
Jericho
Jerusalem
JUDAEA
Machaerus
Hebron
Dead Sea
IDUMEA

Jesus' Ministry Begins

Although Jesus was born in Bethlehem in Judea, his parents lived in Nazareth in Galilee. (Joseph and Mary had to travel down to Bethlehem for a special census required by the Roman authorities.) So it was in Nazareth that Jesus was brought up (Matthew 1, 2).

Nazareth was a small Jewish town, a few miles from the larger non-Jewish city of Sepphoris.

Jesus is baptized

Jesus began preaching soon after John the Baptist appeared, calling on people to repent and warning that the Kingdom of God was near. John was preaching farther south in the Jordan Valley and baptizing people in the river Jordan, probably near the city of Jericho (Luke 3).

Jesus came from Nazareth to hear John and was baptized by him. Soon after his baptism Jesus went into the wilderness – the bare, dry hills above the Dead Sea – and spent forty days there fasting. During this time he was tempted by the devil.

Jesus' message

Jesus then returned to Galilee to begin preaching. John had waited for people to come to him; but Jesus travelled from town to town, from village to village, taking his message of good news. Like John, he preached that the Kingdom of God was at hand and spoke of God's love and forgiveness for those who repented.

Jesus probably started his ministry in the town of Capernaum on the north shore of the Sea of Galilee. In his time, most of its inhabitants would have been involved in fishing or farming.

Jesus went specially to the poor and the diseased, healing many people of diseases such as leprosy and paralysis. He became the friend of fishermen, tax-collectors, and outcasts of society.

The Sermon on the Mount

It was probably from a hill near Capernaum that Jesus preached the Sermon on the Mount. He used many illustrations from farming life – sowing and harvesting, for instance – activities readily seen in the surrounding countryside (Matthew 5–8).

The Sea of Galilee. Inset: Fishing on the Sea of Galilee.

Jesus visited many other nearby towns, such as Bethsaida, northeast of Capernaum, and Chorazin.

Rejected in Nazareth
After preaching in and around Capernaum, Jesus returned to his hometown of Nazareth. But his fellow townspeople did not see him as a religious teacher so much as the son of the local carpenter.

One Sabbath day Jesus preached in the Nazareth synagogue, taking as his Scripture words from the prophet Isaiah:
'The Spirit of the Lord is upon me, because he has anointed me to preach the good news to the poor.'

His listeners were scandalized when Jesus claimed that God cares for and works through Gentiles.

Shock turned to anger, and the men mobbed Jesus out of the synagogue and up a steep hill, intending to throw him from the summit. But Jesus was able to escape and made his way back to Capernaum (Luke 4).

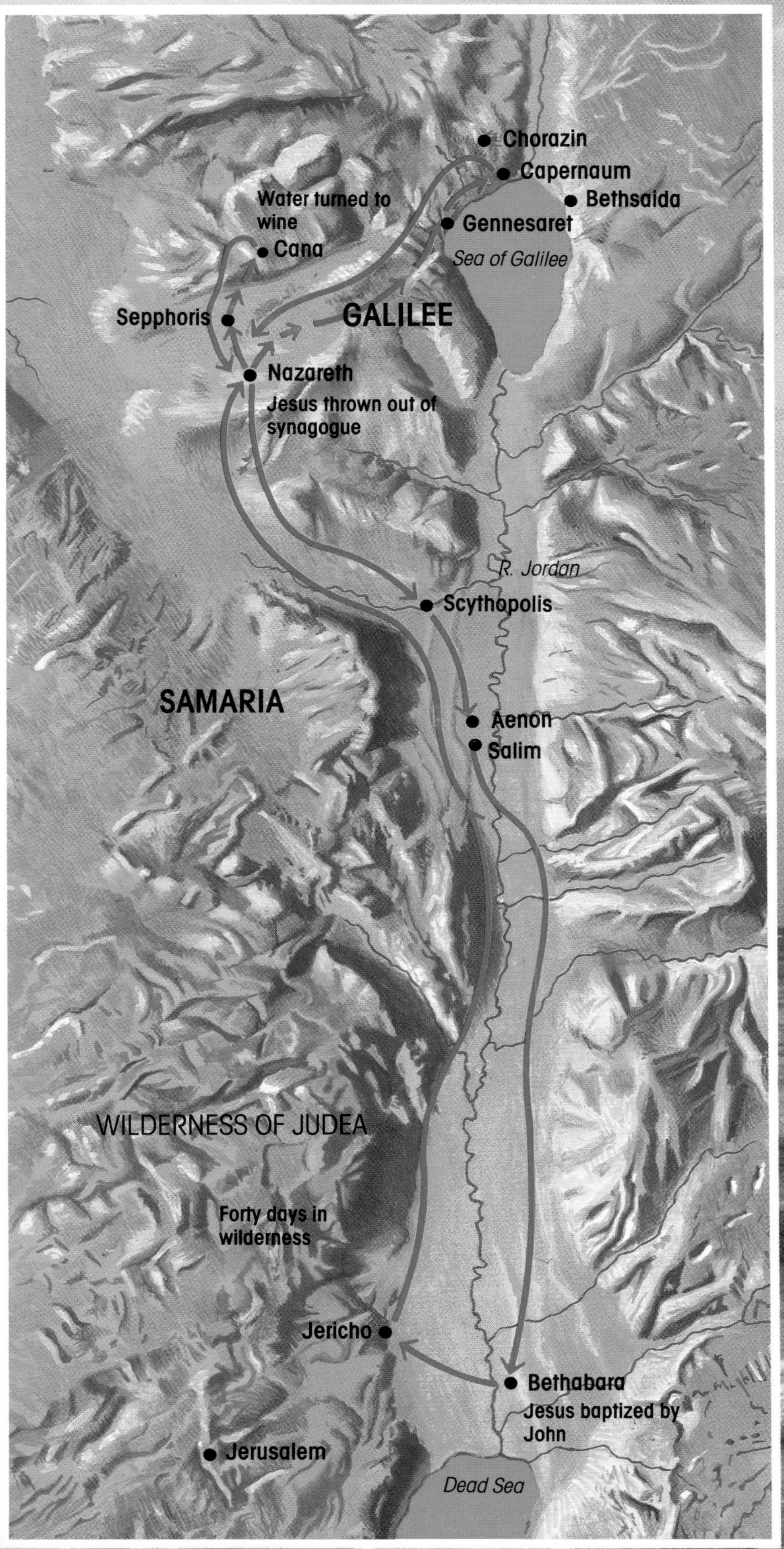

Jesus' Later Ministry

Jesus escapes Herod
When Jesus heard that John the Baptist had been beheaded by Herod Antipas, he left Galilee, travelling north toward the coastal towns of Tyre and Sidon, in what is now Lebanon.

After spending time there, Jesus led his disciples to Caesarea Philippi, Philip's capital. Here, too, they were safe from Herod Antipas.

It was on the road to Caesarea Philippi that there came a turning-point in Jesus' ministry. He asked his disciples : 'Who do you think I am?' It was the impetuous Peter who said: 'You are the Messiah.'

Once Peter had said this, Jesus stopped preaching openly to large crowds. He kept his words for his special followers.

A farmer scatters seed.

The Transfiguration
Just six days later, Jesus took Peter, James, and John to the top of a high mountain. Suddenly they saw him transformed into a shining figure and talking to two other shining figures – Elijah and Moses.

Although traditionally the Transfiguration is believed to have taken place on Mount Tabor, which rises dramatically from the Plain of Esdraelon, it is more likely that it took place on Mount Hermon, which is very close to Caesarea Philippi. Mount Hermon is more than 8,000 feet (2,400 metres) high and capped with snow for much of the year (Mark 6–8).

Jesus travels to Jerusalem
A little later, Jesus set out for Jerusalem. He spent time there healing and teaching; but his actions and words once more caused offence, especially to the religious leaders.

At the Festival of the Dedication Jesus spoke in one of the courts of the Temple. Some people were so shocked that they shouted: 'Blasphemy!' and started to stone him. Jesus also foretold that the Temple would be destroyed: 'There will not be left one stone upon another that will not be thrown down!'

Jesus and his disciples now left Jerusalem again. They crossed the river Jordan and stayed at a place near where Jesus had been baptized. Here Jesus taught his disciples more about his coming suffering and death.

Jesus and Lazarus
Jesus' friends Mary and Martha sent a message to Jesus from their home in Bethany asking him to come because their brother Lazarus was sick. Jesus delayed leaving and arrived to find Lazarus dead and buried. But Jesus restored his friend to life (John 10, 11).

Now Jesus travelled secretly to Ephraim, in the Judean Wilderness, between Bethel and Jericho. He knew what faced him if he returned to Jerusalem – the opposition of the Jewish leaders, the might of the Roman authorities.

Finally Jesus was ready to go to Jerusalem. He travelled down the Jordan valley, passing through Jericho, where he met the little tax-collector Zacchaeus.

The triumphal entry
Jesus and his followers climbed the steep road from Jericho to Jerusalem. When he reached the Mount of Olives, from which he could see the whole city of Jerusalem, Jesus sent disciples to borrow a donkey.

Jesus rode the donkey into Jerusalem and was greeted by crowds shouting: 'Hosanna to the Son of David! Blessed be the King who comes in the name of the Lord!'
Although some Pharisees asked Jesus to silence the crowd, Jesus refused.

After this noisy entry to the city, Jesus left again and spent the night with his friends in Bethany.

Cleansing the Temple
The next morning Jesus re-entered the city and went to the Temple. He drove the dishonest traders and money-changers from the Temple courts, speaking the words of the prophet Jeremiah:
'My house shall be called
A house of prayer for all nations
But you have made it a den of thieves.'

This was the last straw for the chief priests and scribes. They were determined to put a stop to Jesus' activities, though they dared not arrest him publicly, since he was so popular with the people (Mark 10, 11).

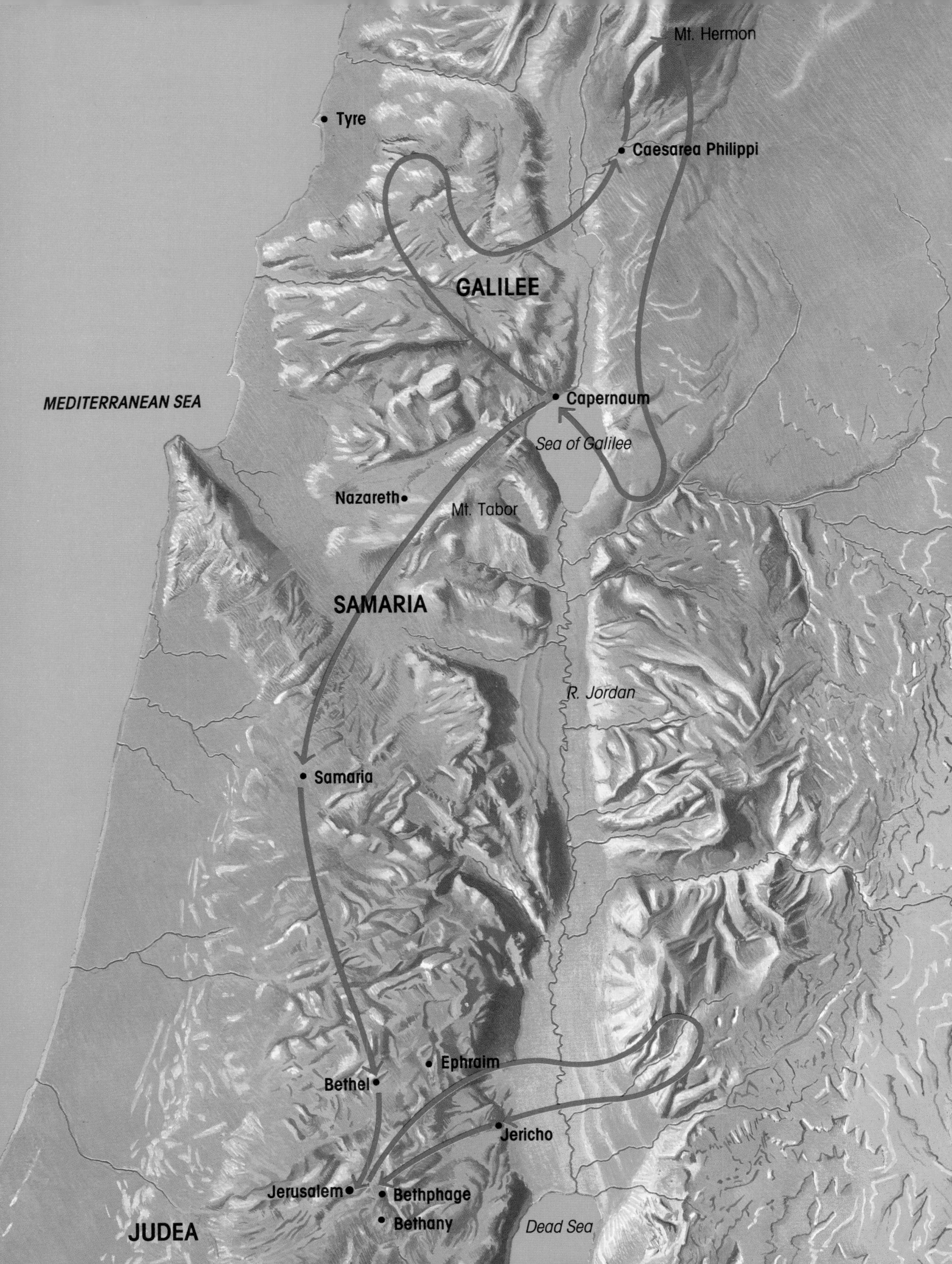

Mt. Hermon
Tyre
Caesarea Philippi
GALILEE
MEDITERRANEAN SEA
Capernaum
Sea of Galilee
Nazareth
Mt. Tabor
SAMARIA
R. Jordan
Samaria
Ephraim
Bethel
Jericho
Jerusalem
Bethphage
Bethany
JUDEA
Dead Sea

Jesus' Death and Resurrection

Jesus and his disciples ate the Last Supper together in a secret place – in the upper room of the Jerusalem house of a friend. By tradition, this house was in the southwest part of the city.

Jesus' Last Night in Jerusalem

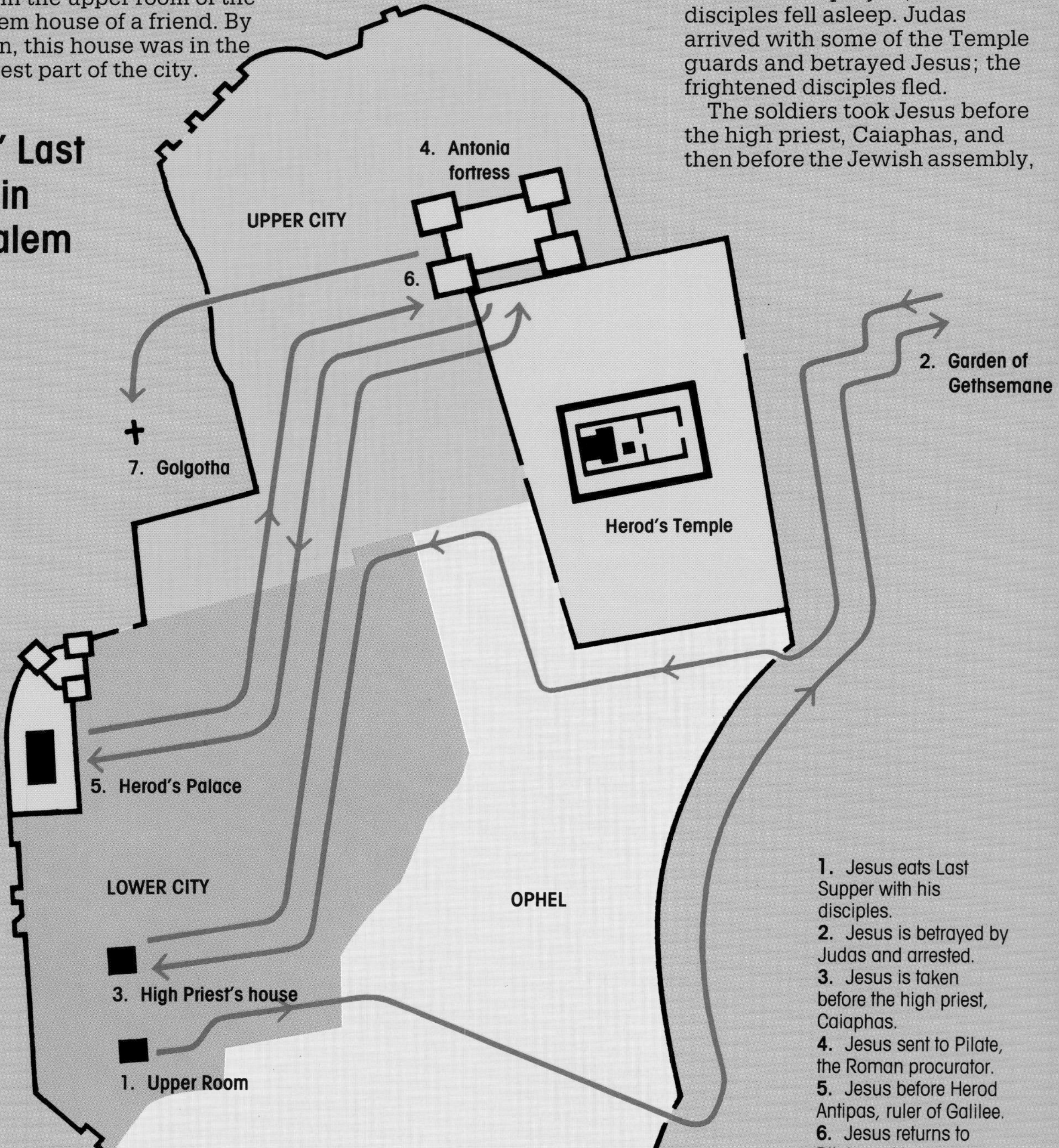

1. Jesus eats Last Supper with his disciples.
2. Jesus is betrayed by Judas and arrested.
3. Jesus is taken before the high priest, Caiaphas.
4. Jesus sent to Pilate, the Roman procurator.
5. Jesus before Herod Antipas, ruler of Galilee.
6. Jesus returns to Pilate and is condemned to death.
7. Jesus is crucified and buried outside the city.

Jesus betrayed

During the meal Judas left to carry out his plans to betray Jesus. Afterwards, Jesus took the disciples out of the city and across the Kidron valley to the Garden of Gethsemane, on the Mount of Olives.

Here Jesus prayed, while his disciples fell asleep. Judas arrived with some of the Temple guards and betrayed Jesus; the frightened disciples fled.

The soldiers took Jesus before the high priest, Caiaphas, and then before the Jewish assembly, or Sanhedrin. When Jesus agreed that he was the Christ, the Son of God, they found him guilty of blasphemy. But they did not have the power to pronounce the death sentence and therefore sent Jesus to Pontius Pilate, the Roman procurator, who was in Jerusalem for the Passover festival.

Jesus condemned

When Pilate realized that Jesus was from Galilee, he sent him to Herod Antipas, also in Jerusalem. Jesus refused to speak, and Antipas mocked him before sending him back to Pilate.

Pilate did not believe Jesus had done anything deserving death and suggested releasing him; but a crowd had gathered and called instead for the release of a condemned murderer named Barabbas.

Jesus was condemned to death outside Pilate's palace. When morning came, he was marched out of the city to a hill called Golgotha (skull) where he was crucified.

When they were quite sure he was dead, the soldiers allowed Jesus' body to be taken down from the cross. It was buried in the tomb of a rich Jew named Joseph of Arimathea (Matthew 27; Mark 14; Luke 23; John 13, 18).

But the story did not end there. Jesus rose from the grave and appeared to many of his followers in many different places:

1. Mary Magdalene met Jesus at the tomb in the garden. At first she mistook him for the gardener (Mark 16:9–11; John 20:11–18).

2. Mary Magdalene and the 'other' Mary met Jesus near the tomb (Matthew 28:9–10).

3. Jesus appeared to the disciples as they were eating in the upper room in Jerusalem. He let them touch him, and he ate with them. He also appeared specially to Thomas and invited him to touch his wounds (Mark 16:14–18; Luke 24:36–49; John 20:19–29).

4. Jesus appeared to Cleopas and another follower on the road to Emmaus, accompanying them to their house (Mark 16:12–13; Luke 24:13–35).

5. Jesus appeared in Galilee to the eleven disciples (Judas had killed himself) on the hill to which he had told them to go (Matthew 28:16–20).

6. Jesus appeared to Peter, James, John, Thomas, Nathanael, and others as they cooked breakfast beside the Sea of Galilee (John 21:1–22).

7. Jesus ascended to heaven from the Mount of Olives, in full view of his disciples (Luke 24:50–1; Acts 1:6–11).

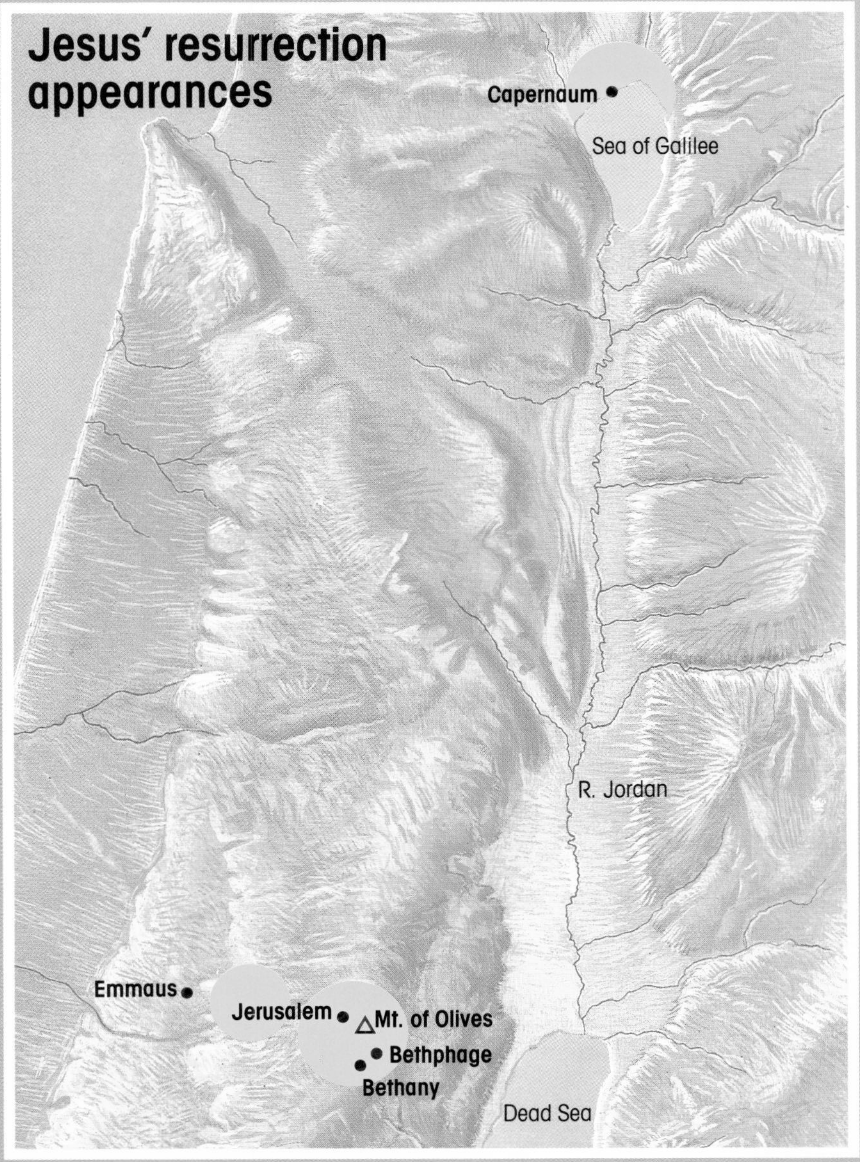

Jesus' resurrection appearances

Capernaum
Sea of Galilee
R. Jordan
Emmaus
Jerusalem
Mt. of Olives
Bethphage
Bethany
Dead Sea

A rolling stone guards the entrance to the family tomb of the Herods.

Paul's Journeys

As Jesus' followers in Jerusalem grew in number, opposition to them grew too. One of their most fearless preachers was Stephen. After a summary trial he was stoned to death by the Jews. Stephen's death marked the onset of persecution of believers. But this only helped spread the gospel. Followers of Jesus fled from Jerusalem, taking with them the good news.

In this way the gospel soon reached Samaria, the Mediterranean coast, Damascus, Phoenicia, the island of Cyprus, and as far as Antioch.

Saul's conversion

The death of Stephen also probably affected Saul, a devout Jew who watched the stoning. Saul was on his way to Damascus to set about persecuting believers there when he had a vision of Christ. As a result he was converted, baptized, and began to preach the gospel (Acts 9).

Saul, now renamed Paul, returned to Jerusalem, where he met the apostle Peter, and Barnabas, a Christian from Cyprus whom he accompanied to Antioch to help preach the good news there. Successful in their mission to Antioch, Paul and Barnabas next set out on a missionary journey to Cyprus and parts of Asia Minor (modern Turkey), much of it through wild,

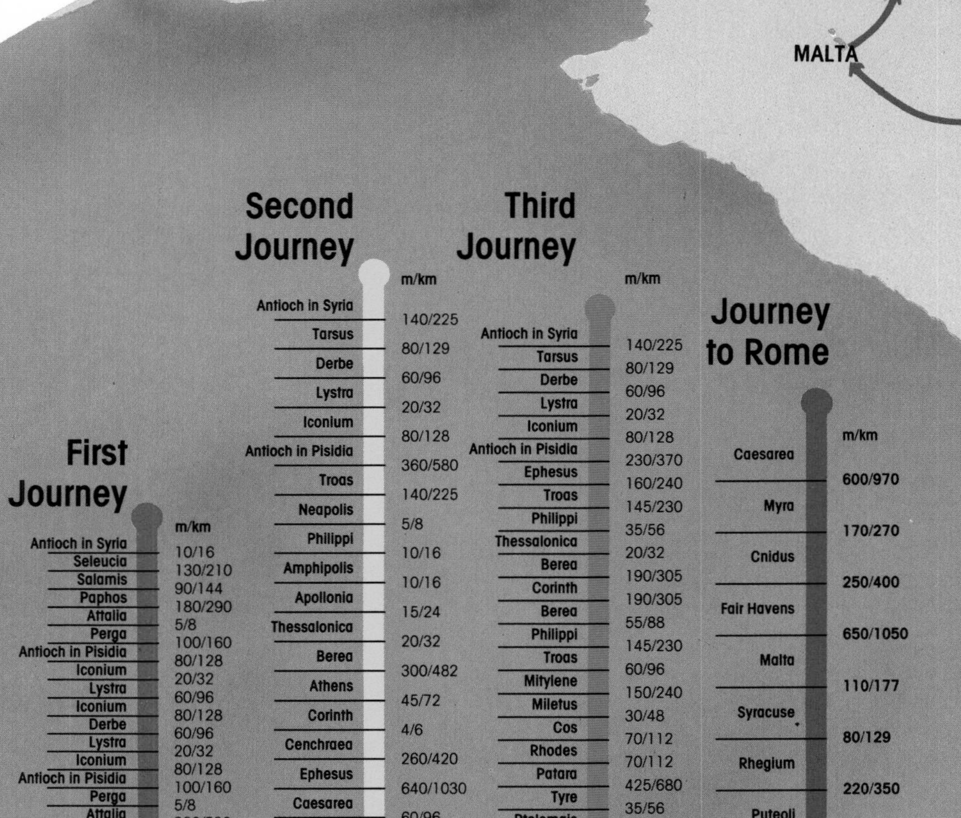

All distances are approximate

mountainous country. They always preached first in the Jewish synagogue and only then to the Gentiles (Acts 13, 14).

After this first missionary journey, Paul returned to Jerusalem to discuss how pagans could become Christian. After much debate, it was agreed that Gentiles could be converted to Christianity without also becoming Jews.

Paul and Barnabas planned a second missionary journey, but when they disagreed about who should accompany them, they parted. Paul took with him a man named Silas, and later a young man called Timothy joined them. After travelling through Asia Minor again, they crossed the Aegean Sea into Europe, taking the gospel to Macedonia and Greece (Acts 15–18).

On the third journey Paul travelled alone, revisiting many places and staying in the great city of Ephesus in Asia Minor for two years (Acts 18–20).

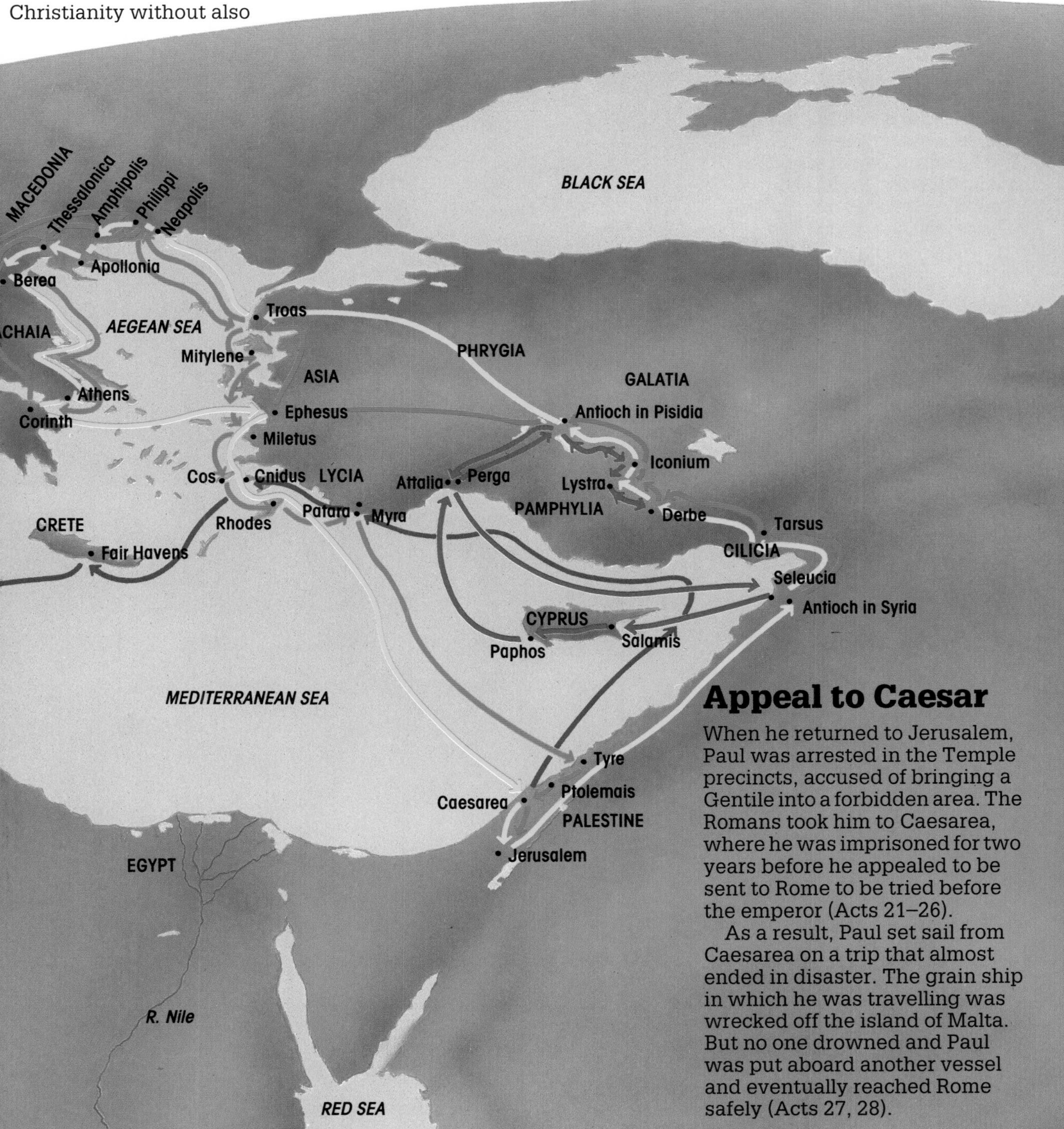

Appeal to Caesar

When he returned to Jerusalem, Paul was arrested in the Temple precincts, accused of bringing a Gentile into a forbidden area. The Romans took him to Caesarea, where he was imprisoned for two years before he appealed to be sent to Rome to be tried before the emperor (Acts 21–26).

As a result, Paul set sail from Caesarea on a trip that almost ended in disaster. The grain ship in which he was travelling was wrecked off the island of Malta. But no one drowned and Paul was put aboard another vessel and eventually reached Rome safely (Acts 27, 28).

The First Churches

The church continued to grow and spread. Although there is a tradition that Paul was beheaded by the emperor Nero in AD 64, it is also possible that he made at least two more journeys, including a trip westward to Spain. We know that Paul wanted to visit Spain.

The fall of Jerusalem

Meanwhile in Jerusalem the fiercely independent Zealots, still bitterly opposed to Roman rule, broke into open revolt in AD 66. The Romans sent general Vespasian, and later his son Titus, to quell the rebellion, which they did with Roman thoroughness and harshness.

After putting down rebel forces in different parts of Palestine, the Romans besieged Jerusalem itself, finally capturing the city in AD 70. The Temple was burned to the ground and most of the city flattened.

The Jewish Christians left Jerusalem when the revolt began, many fleeing to Pella in Transjordan.

The book of Revelation

John, a prisoner on the little island of Patmos in the Aegean Sea, wrote a letter to seven churches in Asia Minor, with a special message for each church, and his prophecy of the fall of Rome and vision of the New Jerusalem. His writings form our book of Revelation.

All seven churches to which John wrote were situated on Roman roads used by postal

Ruins of the Temple of Athene, Pergamum.

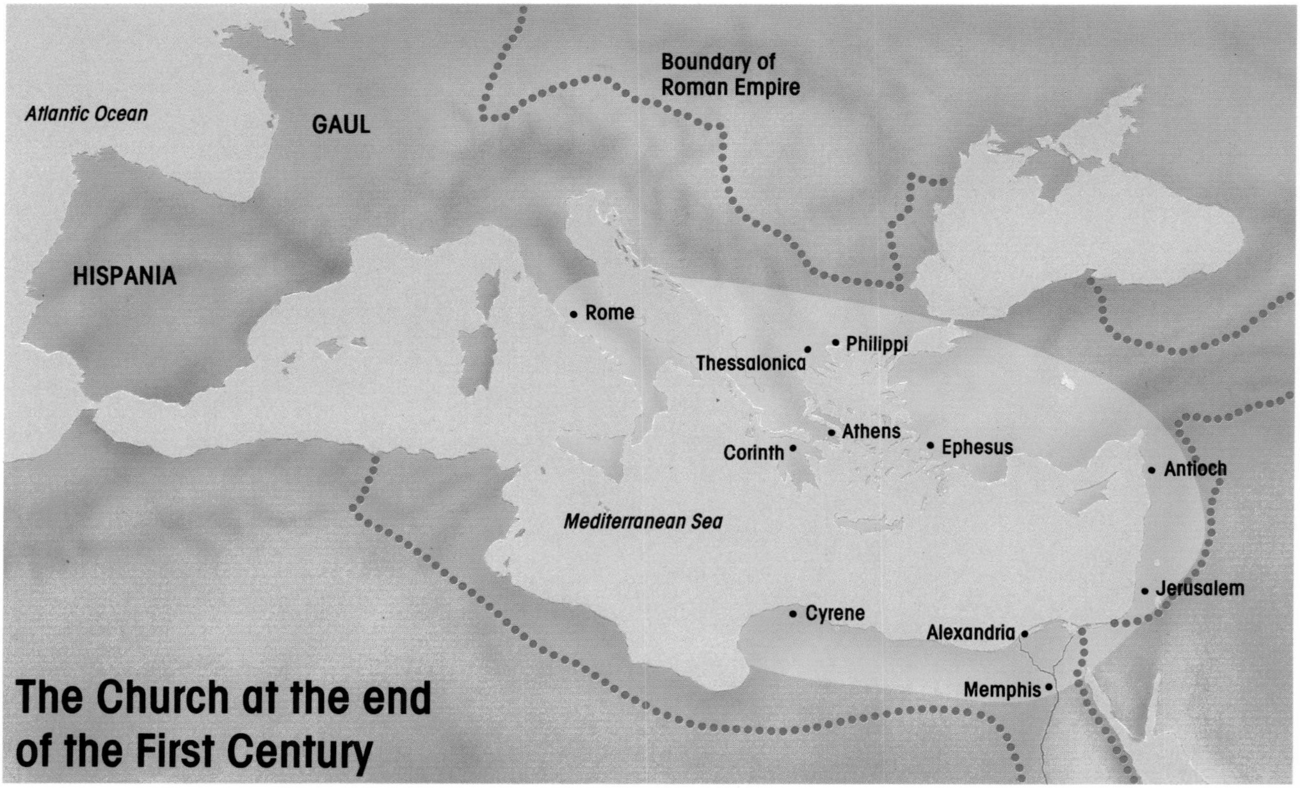

Boundary of Roman Empire
Atlantic Ocean
GAUL
HISPANIA
Rome
Philippi
Thessalonica
Athens
Corinth
Ephesus
Antioch
Mediterranean Sea
Jerusalem
Cyrene
Alexandria
Memphis

The Church at the end of the First Century

couriers. If a courier had arrived at Ephesus by sea from Patmos, he could have travelled north to Smyrna and Pergamum and then east along the Roman road to Thyatira, Sardis, Philadelphia, and Laodicea.

The church spreads
Paul was not the only Christian to found new churches, though he was the most active. From Ephesus he sent Christians into Asia to set up churches at Colossae, Hierapolis and Laodicea (Colossians 4). There were also Christians at Troas, Miletus, and probably Assos; and other missionaries must have founded churches in Pontus, Cappadocia and Bithynia (1 Peter 1).

We know that by the end of the first century the Christian gospel was being preached in places as far apart as North Africa, Spain, and Gaul. There is also an early tradition that it had been carried even to India.

By this time major Christian centres had arisen at Alexandria and Antioch in the east and at Ephesus, Corinth, and Rome in the west.

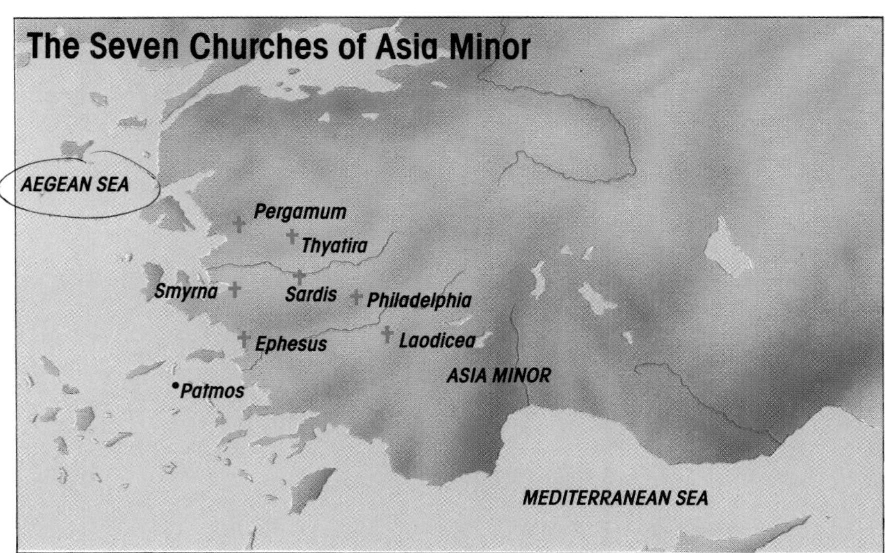

Below: The Temple of Apollo, Corinth.

Triumphant Romans carry off the seven-branched candlestick from the Temple; from the Arch of Titus, Rome.

Bible Places

Antioch in Syria
The third largest city of the Roman Empire. Believers fled here from Jerusalem after the death of Stephen. It was here that they were first called 'Christians'.

Athens
Famous Greek centre of learning, visited by Paul on his second missionary journey.

Beersheba
The most southerly town of the Israelites, sited on the edge of the Negev desert. Specially associated with Abraham, Isaac, and Jacob.

Bethel
A town a few miles north of Jerusalem. Here Jacob had his dream of a ladder to heaven and named it 'Bethel' – house of God.

Bethlehem
Town south of Jerusalem near to which Rachel was buried. Ruth and Naomi settled here, and it became known as the City of David, since David was born here. Centuries later Jesus was born to Mary in Bethlehem.

The Cave of Machpelah, Hebron.

The Parthenon, Athens.

Beth Shan
An ancient city near the Valley of Jezreel. At the Conquest, the Israelites failed to drive out the Canaanites. Saul and Jonathan's bodies hung here after the battle of Gilboa.

Caesarea
Mediterranean port built by Herod the Great. The Roman procurators lived here, and it was here that Paul was tried and imprisoned before being sent to Rome.

Caesarea Philippi
Town near Mount Hermon and near the source of the river Jordan. It was near here too that Peter first acknowledged Jesus as Messiah.

Capernaum
Town on the northwest shore of Lake Galilee. Jesus' headquarters while he was teaching in Galilee and site of many of his miracles.

Corinth
Greek port on the isthmus between the Aegean and Adriatic seas. Paul stayed here for eighteen months during his second missionary journey and wrote at least two letters to the Christians here.

Damascus
The capital of Syria and home of Naaman, who came to Elisha for healing. Saul was on his way here when he was converted.

Ephesus
The most important Roman city of Asia Minor. Paul visited Ephesus on his second missionary journey and stayed here for two years on his third journey. Paul wrote his letters to the church at Corinth from here and later wrote to the Christians at Ephesus.

Galilee
An area and a lake in northern Palestine. The area is hilly and in Jesus' time was crossed by Roman roads. The Sea of Galilee was surrounded by towns, many of them visited by Jesus.

Gibeon
A town a few miles north of Jerusalem. The Gibeonites tricked Joshua into a peace treaty; later the Tent of Meeting was kept here.

Gomorrah
City in the Jordan valley near the Dead Sea. With Sodom, it was destroyed for its wickedness.

Haran
Town in what is now southeast Turkey. Abraham's father, Terah, settled here after leaving Ur; Isaac and Jacob both returned to Haran for a time.

Hazor
Canaanite city defeated by the Israelites. Solomon rebuilt and strengthened Hazor, but it was destroyed by Assyria in the eighth century BC.

Hebron
Town in the Judean hills south of Jerusalem. Abraham often camped near here. David made Hebron his capital before capturing Jerusalem.

Mount Hermon
Mountain on the borders of modern Israel, Lebanon, and Syria, more than 8,000 feet (2,400 metres) high. It marked the northern frontier of Israel and may have been the mountain where Jesus was transfigured.

Model of Jerusalem in the time of Christ.

Jericho
City west of the river Jordan and the world's lowest inhabited place. Joshua won his first victory in the Promised Land by taking Jericho.

Jerusalem
Capital city of David and Solomon and of the kings of Judah. Sited in the Judean hills. David took Jerusalem from the Jebusites and made it his capital. Solomon built palaces and the Temple here.

The Babylonians captured Jerusalem and the Temple in 586 BC. When some of the Jews returned, they rebuilt the Temple and the city walls. Herod the Great later restored and extended the Temple. Jesus visited Jerusalem for the festivals and was tried, crucified, and rose from the grave here. After the Jewish Revolt, Jerusalem and the Temple were destroyed by the Romans in AD 70.

Jezreel
Plain in northern Israel and site of many important battles.

Jordan, river
Main river of Palestine, flowing from Mount Hermon in the north southward to the Dead Sea. Joshua led the Israelites across the Jordan into the Promised Land; John the Baptist baptized many, including Jesus, in its waters.

Megiddo
Important city on the edge of the Plain of Esdraelon, site of many decisive battles. Joshua defeated the king of Megiddo; Solomon made it one of his strongholds. Megiddo has given its name to Armageddon, the last battle.

Nazareth
Town in Galilee where Jesus grew up. He was mobbed out of the synagogue in Nazareth.

Nineveh
Important Assyrian city, especially under King Sennacherib. The prophet Jonah went to Nineveh to save it.

Philippi
Town near the coast of Macedonia, visited by Paul during his second missionary journey. Paul established the first church in Europe here and later wrote a letter to the Philippian Christians.

Rome
Capital of the Roman Empire. Paul came to Rome as a prisoner after he appealed to Caesar. He wrote the great letter to the Roman Christians. By tradition Paul and Peter were both martyred in Rome.

Samaria
Capital city of the northern kingdom, Israel. Samaria was built by kings Omri and Ahab but captured by the Assyrians in 722/1 BC, when the Jews were taken into captivity. In New Testament times the Samaritans were despised by the Jews.

Shechem
Ancient Canaanite city north of Jerusalem, near Mount Gerizim. Abraham stopped here on his journey to Canaan; Joshua gathered the tribes of Israel here after the conquest of Canaan.

Index